Contents

Meeting Special Needs in Mainstream Schools

a Practical Guide for Teachers

Richard Stakes and Garry Hornby

David Fulton Publishers
London

David Fulton Publishers Ltd
2 Barbon Close, London WC1N 3JX

First published in Great Britain by
David Fulton Publishers 1996

British Library Cataloguing in Publication Data

A catalogue record for this book is available from the British Library

ISBN 1–85346–448–1

Typeset by The Harrington Consultancy, London
Printed in Great Britain by the Cromwell Press Ltd, Melksham

Introduction

The purpose of this book is to provide basic information which will be of value to teachers working with pupils with special educational needs (SEN) in mainstream schools. Its aim is to provide practical help and guidance in the organisation and management of classroom provision in an area of education which has been the subject of considerable change in the last few years.

The Code of Practice on the Identification and Assessment of Special Educational Needs (DfE, 1994b) detailed eight different types of SEN. These are: learning difficulties, specific learning difficulties, emotional and behavioural difficulties, physical disabilities, hearing difficulties, visual difficulties, speech and language difficulties and medical conditions. The nature of these difficulties and their severity can vary widely, as can the way in which they are revealed.

The causes are varied and complex. They can be set in a framework of personal difficulties manifested by children in the school setting, and placed in the context of learning, physical, emotional and social difficulties. These vary from those which are easily observable (e.g. very poor reading skills), to those which are much less obvious (colour blindness) and those which are much more debatable (factors relating to socio-economic circumstances). This situation can be further compounded in that a difficulty which appears as a major problem in school for one child may not be so for another in an apparently similar situation.

It is not the purpose of this book to discuss the underlying causes of SEN in any detail. This has been undertaken extensively in previous publications, some of which are referred to here. Rather, it will concentrate on practical classroom strategies and activities to aid the development of competent teachers who have little or no previous experience of working with these pupils.

Recent trends indicate the need for the development of a competence-based approach for all teachers. This has emerged specifically in relation to those working with pupils with SEN. The Teacher Training Agency (TTA, 1994) and the Special Educational Needs Training Consortium (SENTC, 1996) have argued the value of this approach. The documentation from both OFSTED and the TTA (1994) indicate that newly qualified teachers should have gained certain skills as part of their training. These are extensive, ranging over twenty-seven different competences.

An analysis by Reynolds (1992) placed the skills needed by new teachers into seven categories. These included:

- planning lessons at an appropriate level to link prior knowledge to new learning;
- developing a rapport and positive interaction with pupils;
- establishing fair and appropriate rules and routines;
- managing classrooms to promote the learning of academic tasks;
- assessing pupil learning in a variety of ways;

- adapting teaching strategies according to the results;
- reflecting both critically and positively on personal performance and that of pupils.

This book aims to facilitate the development of these skills. It will identify key issues in the organisation and delivery of provision for children with SEN in mainstream schools. Through discussion and analysis it will provide useful and up-to-date information for the classroom teacher working with such pupils. The approach which has been taken is to divide the knowledge base on special education into thirteen chapters.

Chapter 1 discusses several background issues related to SEN, particularly the effects of the Warnock Report (DES, 1978), the requirements of the Code of Practice (DfE, 1994b) and the use of statements of special educational need.

Chapter 2 is concerned with the characteristics of children with learning difficulties. It discusses in particular the intellectual, social, emotional and familial factors that can affect the performance of children in school.

Chapters 3 and 4 are concerned with teaching children with a variety of sensory and physical difficulties increasingly found among those attending mainstream schools. These chapters seek to provide essential information and to indicate where further details might be found.

Chapter 5 is concerned with the key practical classroom considerations of teaching pupils with SEN. Topics covered include differentiation, setting homework and liaison with other staff and professionals.

Chapter 6 is concerned with the assessment of pupils' needs to produce sound teaching programmes. This includes discussions on the value of both informal and formal assessments as well as information on selecting appropriate assessment materials. It concentrates particularly on assessment issues relating to reading skills.

Chapter 7 is concerned with curriculum planning issues. Issues covered include the importance of planning, deciding priorities, the effect of the requirements of the National Curriculum and the relationship between planning for pupils with SEN and the developmental stages of learning outlined by Piaget.

Chapter 8 looks at classroom management and behavioural issues. This includes a discussion of both appropriate and inappropriate techniques to use with pupils with SEN.

Chapters 9, 10 and 11 consider key subject areas relating to work done with those with SEN. They concentrate on developing skills in reading, spelling and mathematics.

Chapter 12 relates to working with parents of children with SEN. It concentrates particularly on a model for parental involvement and the value of communications between teachers and parents.

Chapter 13 is concerned with whole-school issues. These include developing a whole-school policy and the use of Individual Education Programmes (IEPs).

The framework for the content of these chapters is set as a model which is defined by four practical questions and a four-point teaching strategy. The questions are:

1. Where do I start?
2. What do I need to know about the child?
3. What does this information tell me?
4. What approaches might I use to help the pupil?

The answers to these questions need to be related to the skills of the teacher. There are a number of basic skill areas that all teachers must address to be effective with pupils with SEN in their classrooms. These can be best summed up as:

- the assessment of children's needs;
- a diagnosis based on the results of these assessments;
- plans of action to help overcome pupils' difficulties;
- a review of both the progress which pupils have made and of the effectiveness of the approaches.

These skills are essential and must underpin the work of successful teachers. Further, they should be used constantly in a cyclical process to evaluate those they teach, perhaps on a lesson-by-lesson basis.

For children with SEN these skills must also be coupled with a considerable emphasis on the development of good pupil–teacher relationships. For so many pupils with such difficulties, forming a strong personal bond is essential for any learning to take place. In some cases this relationship, with its emphasis on mutual respect, may be more important to them than anything that is listed in any curriculum documentation. A simplistic diagram of this approach is shown in Figure 1.

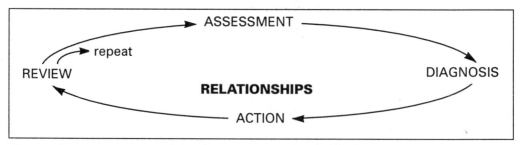

Figure 1 A model showing the principles of effective teaching

There is a considerable body of literature which indicates that without a great deal of thought, imagination and skill based on such an approach by their teachers, many pupils with SEN are likely to become aggressive, disaffected or liable to truant, particularly at the secondary school stage.

The authors wish to acknowledge the assistance of Nessie Wagstaff who read the manuscript and made a number of suggestions which were incorporated into the book.

CHAPTER 1

Overview

INTRODUCTION

This first chapter serves as an overview of the issues which are often contributory factors in determining whether a child has special educational needs. It will concentrate firstly on the legal framework for provision and will detail briefly the effect of the Warnock Report (DES, 1978) and the Code of Practice (DfE, 1994b) as they affect the work of the classroom teacher. It will then indicate, through a brief discussion of the key issues, some of the reasons why special educational provision is needed.

THE CODE OF PRACTICE

The Code of Practice (DfE, 1994b) is described (p.11) as 'a guide for schools and LEAs about the practical help they can give to pupils with special educational needs'. This document makes recommendations as to how schools might encourage the development of good practice in both the organisation of provision for children with SEN and the delivery of the curriculum for them.

It is a step by step approach detailing the requirements for all involved in schools. The document sets out a five stage approach to meeting SEN. It covers the responsibilities of all who work in the school and the governing body, as well as those with responsibilities for pupils with SEN in the LEA.

The Code is a complex document which details procedures at each of the five stages. This chapter will focus on the responsibilities of the class teacher operating at Stage 1 of this approach. At this stage the teacher can 'trigger' what is described (p.14) as 'a registration of concern' to the appropriate member of staff (special needs department, form teacher, head of department or head of year) about a pupil whom they are teaching. It is only at this point that the SEN Coordinator can be asked to help collect and marshal any further information to further identify the needs of the child. Should this procedure be 'triggered' this would be the initial step on the road progressing through the various stages, which for a minority of children will result in a Statement of Special Educational Need at Stage 5.

It is the responsibility of all teachers to be aware of the requirements of the Code in detail. In this respect it is important that they should read and discuss it. For those seeking further information or interpretation the handbook by Hornby, Davis and Taylor (1995) is very useful.

For children of school age the practices and procedures outlined in the Code are underpinned by four key concepts. These are: a *continuum of SEN*, a *continuum of provision*, a *broad, balanced and relevant curriculum* and a *good working partnership with parents*. The continuum of need was a concept detailed in the Warnock Report (DES, 1978) relating to the wide range of difficulties which children experience. These range from mild through to moderate to severe and profound difficulties. This can range at one end to those pupils with SEN who are fully integrated within the mainstream school and who participate fully in the activities offered, to those who are at its other end, who are taught in special schools or outside the school system.

The curricular programme which is offered to pupils with SEN must be set within the National Curriculum and be taught at an appropriate level and pace. For many, particularly those with learning difficulties, this will be considerably different from that of many of their peers.

The partnership with parents of children with SEN is important in a number of ways. Often, because their children have SEN they will need extra support and guidance. Further, they will have information and experiences of their children from outside school which can provide a valuable perspective on their development within it. Parents also have a legal right to be informed of the progress of their children in school. Chapter 12 of this book is devoted to working with parents of children with SEN.

The majority of pupils in mainstream schools will be at Stages 1 to 3 of the Code. Stages 4 and 5 involve the LEA and might lead to a Statement of Special Educational Need. Stages 1 to 3 focus on the policy and provision established in the school, with contributions from the teaching staff, the head teacher and the governing body.

Responsibilities of the class teacher

For the class teacher at Stage 1 there are distinct responsibilities. These include:

- the identification, as early as possible, of children likely to have special educational needs;
- making immediate provision for the teaching and assessment of these pupils;
- informing parents of decisions affecting their child, and developing a partnership with them to help in assessing and planning for the child;
- informing and assisting the school special needs coordinator to collect relevant information about children with SEN.

Other information which is needed at this stage

From the school the information which will have to be collected includes:

- all current and past records relating to the child including those from any other school they have attended in the past year;
- available data from any National Curriculum assessments;
- standardised test results, profiles of attainment or screening test results;
- information contained on their Record of Achievement;
- school based reports from anyone who has had contact with them;

- observations of the child's behaviour;
- health or social problems which are known to the school.

Parents are required to detail additional information with regard to their child's health, behaviour and general development, which might be relevant to their progress. They are also asked their views of the child's progress both at home and at school. Information may also be obtained from other agencies such as the health or social services which may have had dealings with them as well as from the children themselves.

The views of children should also be taken into consideration at this stage. Specifically this relates to personal perceptions of their difficulties and how they would like to be addressed.

THE WARNOCK REPORT

The recommendations made in the Warnock Report (DES, 1978) were instrumental in leading to the integration of as many children as possible, whatever their difficulties, into mainstream schools. This was enhanced by the Education Act 1981 which implemented much of the thinking of the Warnock Committee.

The Warnock Report did not itself initiate an integrationalist philosophy; rather it confirmed the long-term stance taken by many teachers and parents of pupils with SEN, which had been articulated in a variety of forms and in different circumstance throughout much of this century, but with increased fervour throughout the 1960s and 1970s. Essentially what the Report did was to capture the mood of the times, in this respect. The 'spirit of Warnock' as it became known was a key element in the development of provision and the initiation of programmes for this group of pupils throughout the 1980s.

Figures produced in the Warnock Report suggested that around 20 per cent of pupils in schools would need, at some time during their schooling, some form of extra provision to meet their particular educational needs. The Audit Commission Report (Audit Commission/HMI, 1992) indicated that of these pupils some 14 per cent with SEN were being catered for within the ordinary school, while 0.8 per cent received extra help from their Local Education Authority or attended a unit within mainstream schools. Only some 1.3 per cent of pupils attended any separate form of special provision such as special schools.

STATEMENTS OF SPECIAL EDUCATIONAL NEED

Most pupils in special schools in England and Wales are subject to a Statement of Special Educational Need, some pupils in mainstream schools have them also. This is a legally binding document detailing the required educational provision for the pupil as well as the difficulties which the child has. It is determined by the recommendations of interested parties, with contributions from the school, the child's parents, representatives from the local services such as the school psychological service and social services; as well as representation from the LEA.

Statements are reviewed annually so that the changing needs and circumstances of children can be taken into account.

The number of pupils with statements varies widely from school to school. The 1980s saw a rise in the number of pupils placed in special schools. However, since then there has been a gradual fall in the numbers placed there (Audit Commission/HMI, 1992). This has been matched by a corresponding rise in the number of pupils with statements in mainstream schools during this period.

The Audit Commission/HMI Report (1992) also highlighted the considerable variation between the number of pupils with statements in different Local Educational Authorities. The percentage of the total school population with statements varied between 3.2 per cent and 0.8 per cent in different LEAs – a significant difference. This was put down to a lack of clarity of definition of special educational needs by LEAs. For others, such as Mortimore and Blackstone (1982) and Booth *et al.* (1992), social differences and variances in the value placed by parents on formal education were also regarded as important factors.

CHANGES IN THE MAINSTREAM SCHOOL SEN POPULATION

Since the greater emphasis on the integration of children with SEN into mainstream schools not only has the number of these children increased but also the variety of their disabilities. Children with a far wider range of learning difficulties and variety of medical conditions and physical disabilities are now attending mainstream classes. This has implications not only for the children but also for their teachers.

For example, for some children their physical disability is caused by congenital difficulties or by a accident earlier in their lives. This can make learning in the mainstream school classroom more difficult for them than the rest of their peers. For others their difficulties relate to intellectual problems, such as retaining information or concentrating on required classroom tasks for any length of time. Because of this their overall intellectual development may be slower than many of those around them.

The increased integration of children with SEN has occurred, to no small measure, because of the prevailing philosophy subscribed to by many teachers and parents of those with SEN that, on social grounds at least, this group benefits greatly from long-term contact with the rest of their age group.

IDENTIFYING DIFFICULTIES

For pupils with physical or sensory difficulties sometimes the nature of the problem is clearly recognisable. A difficulty with movement is an example of this. In other circumstances, e.g. hearing loss, this will not always be the case and it may not be obvious to the teacher that the child has a problem at all. Without this information teachers will not always be aware that they may have to make adjustments to accommodate the needs of the child.

A learning difficulty may not be as easy to recognise as a physical or sensory disability. Often there are no outward signs to help the teacher. Children with learning difficulties may seem, superficially at least, no different from their more able counterparts. Even sophisticated patterns of speech and an ability to answer questions aloud in class may not be accompanied with an ability to read well or to write or spell accurately.

Pupils with learning difficulties will often leave the teacher with no idea as to why they are experiencing problems. The only obvious feature is that the child is unable to perform certain tasks set by the teacher as adequately as others in the class. The probable reasons need to be investigated in order to account for these difficulties. Among the more important are:

- an overall low level of intelligence which makes learning more difficult;
- verbal intelligence without the corresponding literacy skills;
- a lack of competence and/or confidence with other core skills;
- social or cultural factors making the school environment difficult for the child to perform well in school;
- inadequate learning strategies.

Whatever the causation, by the time they reach the upper stages of the primary school let alone in the secondary school, children may react to the demands made by their teachers by being resentful, frustrated, depressed or perhaps are left with a feeling of inferiority. Teachers must therefore show both awareness and empathy for the difficulties experienced by such pupils. They need to be keenly aware of the needs of pupils with SEN, and provide for them individually as part of their normal daily work.

CHAPTER TWO

The characteristics of children with learning difficulties

INTRODUCTION

There is considerable evidence from educational research and anecdotal sources to illustrate the considerable negative impact that experiencing learning difficulties at school can have on children. Stakes (1987), when interviewing pupils with learning difficulties in the last year of their secondary education mainstream schools, found that many of them had considerably more negative feelings than the rest of their peer group and were resigned to failure. Cooper (1994), through research which involved interviewing disaffected pupils, found strong feelings of a lack of interest and total rejection of anything that was in any way connected with school.

Others have put these feelings into a much wider context – arguing that to the disillusioned pupil the teacher was another type of policeman, school another type of imprisonment and work which they have to do as meaningless. Bearing this in mind it is important that the practising teacher is able to clearly identify the features of children with learning difficulties. This will provide them with information which may help them towards a greater awareness of the difficulties.

DEFINITION OF LEARNING DIFFICULTIES

The Code of Practice (1994) described learning difficulties in relation to the acquisition of basic skills by children. It indicated that children with SEN will have difficulties in acquiring literacy and numeracy skills compared with their peers.

For many children in mainstream schools these difficulties may only be mild and slow down their overall pace of learning. Other children may have more complex difficulties which may affect other areas of their learning, such as their social skills. Certain children will have specific difficulties which affect only one part of their learning development such as spelling or reading. A small number of children have profound learning problems, often accompanied by secondary disabilities. Most of these children are educated outside mainstream schools.

IDENTIFYING PUPILS

The features which may help to identify children with learning difficulties fall into seven basic categories. These are:

- academic work
- school record
- intellectual characteristics
- physical appearance
- social factors
- emotional factors
- family background.

Three important points need to be made when considering this issue:

1. The points made in this section cannot be taken in isolation. They need to be considered and discussed in conjunction with those made in other chapters in the book.
2. All the points made in this book are not exhaustive.
3. Because a child may show one, or even a number of characteristics from the lists provided, this will not necessarily mean that they will have learning problems.

These are some of the problems associated with any list such as those which follow. Therefore great care should be taken when using such a list. Nevertheless, despite these points, such a list can be a useful starting point, and perhaps the items on it can best be used as a check-list for individual children in order to provide a personal profile. For this reason elaboration of each of the seven factors follows.

ACADEMIC WORK

Children with learning difficulties may:

- have difficulty in reading, writing, spelling, arithmetic;
- avoid 'academic' tasks;
- seek out the routine jobs around the classroom – tidying up, giving out the books, cleaning the classroom;
- prefer practical lessons;
- not be interested in books or reading;
- need supervision when doing routine tasks;
- always ask for help/never ask for help;
- make mistakes in copying;
- be slow to carry out a task, never finish a piece of work;
- say they have finished a piece of work (especially written work) very quickly, but having done very little of it;
- move from one piece of work to another, trying to pretend they have finished;
- lose equipment such as pencils or books.

SCHOOL RECORD

As far as children's records throughout the school is concerned a number of features may be apparent. If you have concerns about particular pupils it is worth talking to other members of staff to elicit if there is a record of:

- poor performance across other subjects in the curriculum;
- a clumsy approach to PE, woodwork or domestic science;
- a record of 'skipping' lessons;
- a poor attendance record;
- poor reports from previous schools;
- adverse comments made about them by others in the class or year group;
- many changes of school;
- been referred to the school psychological service.

INTELLECTUAL CHARACTERISTICS

Children with learning difficulties often have a distinct lack of awareness of things about them. They can be confused about places on a map or vague in the details of the journey from home to school in anything but oral recall. If these seem to be a feature of children in your class further investigation may be worthwhile. This could include finding out if the children:

- know little about the world around them;
- have limited experiences to draw on;
- show little or no originality in their work generally;
- seem to have few interests;
- are unable to follow simple instructions;
- do not see obvious connections in the work being done, that others in the class can see;
- need lots of help;
- have weak vocabulary skills and a poor speech pattern;
- use single words rather than sentences when speaking;
- rarely contribute to discussions;
- have a desire for inconsequential chatter or a repetitiveness of speech patterns;
- are hyperactive, compared with others in the same class or year group;
- attend to other matters rather than those at hand;
- have a short concentration span.

PHYSICAL APPEARANCE

This is an area of some debate and particular caution must be exercised when investigating this aspect. Despite significant attempts, particularly in the nineteenth century, to link personal appearance and intellectual capacity this is an area which is both fraught with problems and of dubious value. Nevertheless a number of features are worth at least some inspection, particularly if they can be linked to other features outlined in this analysis. In this connection some further investigation should be considered if children:

- are either small in size or grossly oversize for their age;
- have a speech impediment;
- exhibit some evidence of deafness;

- exhibit visual difficulties;
- rub their eyes a lot;
- peer at their work;
- need glasses but do not always wear them;
- lack coordination;
- have writing in which the letters are badly formed;
- have generally messy handwriting;
- produce disorganised work which is badly set out;
- are clumsy.

SOCIAL FACTORS

Sometimes children with SEN have difficulties in making strong relationships with other children. Others in their peer groups may have difficulties in making long-lasting relationships with those pupils who they regard as odd, or different from themselves. In this respect some of the social features which may be apparent to the teacher could help to support information gathered from other areas. Particular attention should be paid if children are:

- socially isolated;
- generally mixing with children a lot younger or older than themselves;
- aggressive towards other children;
- excessively affectionate;
- uninhibited in addressing adults;
- having difficulties in making any kind of relationship with their teacher;
- disruptive in class;
- interfering with what other pupils are doing on the playground;
- always on the fringe of activities.

EMOTIONAL FACTORS

Children's difficulties in school with their work or peer group relationships can manifest themselves in a variety of different ways in the classroom. One of these is related to the emotional stability of the child in school. A number of observable features are important in this respect and particular note should be made if children:

- appear emotionally immature;
- have a poor self-image and are concentrating regularly on not being able to do things;
- appear constantly nervous or anxious;
- are demanding of the teacher's time compared with others in the group;
- are restless on many occasions;
- are easily distractible;
- cannot sit still;
- are easily upset;
- stammer;

- bite their fingernails excessively;
- are irritable on a regular basis;
- are generally uncooperative with both the teacher and the class;
- have temper tantrums;
- are often dreamy;
- are often withdrawn;
- are regularly moody.

FAMILY BACKGROUND

The issue of the relationship between children's family background and their performance in school is a complex area which is fraught with problems. Nevertheless noting the behaviour of pupils and their personal circumstances can be of value. However, these must be used with care, and as with some of the issues identified above, not taken in isolation. Particular note should be taken if children:

- have parents who have separated or divorced;
- come from a family where there is unemployment of one of the parents;
- are on free meals;
- are in care;
- have no contact with their natural parents;
- have anxious parents;
- are regularly compared unfavourably with other children in the family;
- are a member of a family which has had children who were of a similar ability in the school before (e.g. weak reading or a poor scholastic record);
- appear to lack care and attention from home;
- have few possessions;
- have no recognition of their birthdays;
- are not taken on holiday or on family outings;
- are poorly clothed.

As can be seen from the information provided above, factors affecting performance in school are wide ranging and often difficult to pin down. The responsibilities of teachers lie in their awareness of the relevant circumstances and their classroom-based observational skills. Initially their key role is to recognise these and then to act in those cases where it is felt there should be further investigation.

CHAPTER 3

Children with hearing and sight difficulties

INTRODUCTION

This chapter will concentrate on the difficulties of children who have either visual or hearing impairments. It will consider such problems as how these manifest themselves, what difficulties can occur in the learning situation and what approaches are most successful for the classroom teacher to employ in order to minimise these.

Increasingly, since the 1981 Education Act, there has been a move towards greater integration of pupils with both sight and hearing difficulties into mainstream schools. The children who have been integrated have a wide range of impairments from relatively mild problems, which may mean that they must sit in a particular part of the room to gain most benefit from their lessons, to those pupils who have considerably greater problems and need the help of specialist teachers and equipment.

There are important consequences for the class teacher when a child with sight problems or a hearing loss is in the classroom and it is important that the consequences for the class teacher are discussed. Of course specialist advice should be obtainable from the Special Educational Needs Coordinator (SENCO) or the SEN department but some basic information about the issues raised by these impairments is essential to good management by the class teacher.

HEARING LOSS

MANIFESTATIONS

Basically there are two types of hearing loss: conductive and sensorineural. The first of these is often caused by a blockage in the ear like wax or 'glue ear' which results from a collection of fluid in the ear when a child has catarrh or a heavy cold. These cases are often treatable medically and hearing can be restored, often to within normal limits. Many young children suffer from these problems which are often accompanied by poor speech, limited vocabulary, poor comprehension of spoken language and difficulties in discriminating and sequencing sounds, as well as problems in listening.

Sensorineural hearing losses are generally caused by difficulties with the nerves which link to the ear. These are more serious, sometimes irreversible. Typically a hearing aid is needed to produce amplification of sound but it is important to realise that this will not restore normal hearing. Depending on the level of loss a hearing aid will help children to discriminate sounds; however, this will be distorted. The number of pupils suffering from this type of difficulty is very small. Figures mentioned by Sherliker (1993) indicated that only some 0.1 per cent of pupils were in this category.

DIFFICULTIES OCCURRING FROM CONDUCTIVE HEARING LOSS

When this type of hearing loss arises children may:

- find listening a difficulty;
- be slower in learning to talk;
- have unclear speech;
- feel insecure and confused in class;
- not hear clearly in a class that is seldom quiet;
- be withdrawn and often wait for cues from other children;
- give the impression of being able to listen on occasions.

THE EFFECT OF SENSORINEURAL HEARING LOSS

With this type of hearing loss most pupils will have difficulty with the higher frequencies of sound used in speech and what they will hear will be unpredictable. In these cases it is important to check what the child has heard. They can have particular difficulties with the more complex structures in the language and of course this will affect their overall understanding.

STRATEGIES TO HELP PUPILS WITH A HEARING LOSS

Webster and Elwood (1985) and Webster and Wood (1989) provide useful information for those working with pupils with hearing difficulties. They suggest that the following points are of importance:

- The use of visual clues to make it clear what is being said.
- The emphasis of important instructions or key words.
- A clear understanding of the introduction to each topic, allowing children time to find out about the topic in advance so that they have some understanding before the lesson begins.
- Writing new vocabulary on the blackboard.
- Trying to give homework instructions at a time when the class is quiet. This will help those with hearing loss.
- Allowing a friend of the child in question to check that the instructions and information are clear.
- Rephrasing as well as repeating phrases and words that have been misunderstood.

- In oral lessons making sure that the pace of the discussion is not too fast for those with hearing difficulties.
- When other children answer, repeating their answers to make sure that those who have difficulty hearing have understood. For some children the ability to lip-read will be a considerable skill, however they cannot do that unless they can see the lips of the person speaking.
- A blacked out room for a TV programme or slides can be an impossible environment for a child who relies on lip-reading.
- Walking about the room can make life difficult for children trying to lip-read. The background noise made by feet will be unhelpful also.
- Not obscuring your face with your hands. Again this will make lip-reading difficult.
- Note taking for these children is very difficult, as is listening to a tape recorder.
- Background noise such as others chatting or the movement of furniture can be very distracting for those using an hearing aid.
- Some sports and outdoor activities will create their own difficulties and dangers. It is critical that safety measures are met and that every child has understood the instructions which have been given.

DIFFICULTIES WITH SIGHT

MANIFESTATIONS

Visual skills, as with hearing skills, are important in so many ways in the learning process. For children with sight problems there can be difficulties in learning to read, in itself a critical factor in success at school. It is the purpose of this chapter to outline these problems and discuss some of the strategies which are available to help alleviate them.

By the time children reach secondary school age most of those who have difficulties with their eyes will have been discovered and some form of remedial action taken. As with hearing, the remedies can vary according to the level of impairment and teachers should be aware that for some pupils with relatively severe problems special arrangements need to be made. Normally the school will be aware of those pupils in this category and the SENCO will inform the rest of the staff in the school.

WHAT TO LOOK OUT FOR

Chapman and Stone (1988) and Best (1992) indicated that children with sight problems may display a number of characteristics. These include:

- clumsiness;
- poor hand–eye coordination;
- holding the head in an unusual way;

- frowning, making faces or squinting more often than normally sighted children;
- complaining of headaches or dizziness;
- having poorly formed handwriting;
- having difficulty in seeing the blackboard;
- becoming more tired and needing more breaks.

If children display a number of these characteristics, particularly difficulties in seeing work on the blackboard, it is worth checking with someone else in the school to see if there is a recognised sight problem. In a number of cases, for a variety of reasons children can be reluctant to wear glasses and attempt to hide their difficulties. Initially, if there is thought to be a problem this is one aspect worth checking on.

THE CONSEQUENCES FOR LEARNING

It is worth making a number of points here relating both to teaching technique and to classroom organisation.

It is common practice for a teacher to move around the classroom during a lesson. There are strong disciplinary reasons for doing this. However, for those pupils with sight difficulties this movement can be very distracting and a teacher may need to consciously limit the amount of movement to that which is essential. Similarly children with difficulties in this area can have problems with the number of visual stimuli that they have to deal with in a lesson. Constant eye movement between the blackboard, the teacher, a textbook and an exercise book may cause severe difficulties. Teachers should bear this in mind and try to plan their lessons accordingly.

Vision is used by us all as a major learning tool and for pupils with sight problems learning can be a slower process than for the rest of us. They may, for example, not be able to see the detail that children with good sight are able to, or perhaps they may take longer to assimilate the information. The need to allow a greater length of time should be borne in mind.

As has already been mentioned, reading can cause problems for children with visual difficulties. Sometimes it is necessary to increase the size of the print in a book or photocopied worksheet to enable pupils to see them more easily. For others it is the paper that is used which causes the difficulties – in these cases matt white paper can be better to read from than glossy paper which reflects light.

Poor formation of letters when completing written work has already been mentioned as a possible sign of sight problems. This can be compounded by poor hand–eye coordination. For some children a sloping surface can prove to be a better approach for developing their skills. Time may also be needed to experiment with the tool best suited for writing, the size of the lines on the paper as well as finding the best position in the classroom for seeing the blackboard.

Where circumstances allow, children with visual difficulties can benefit from the lesson being taped so that they can listen to it later and absorb the information at their own speed.

Careful, clear labelling of materials and displays in the classroom can help visually impaired pupils. Similarly, keeping corridors and the aisles between desks and tables, without obstructions, is essential to the easy movement of pupils.

Both sunlight and artificial lighting can in certain circumstances cause problems. Problems will vary according to the type of visual loss and advice needs to be sought on this issue from specialist teachers to develop the best approach for each individual case.

For children with certain difficulties there is a need for them to use typewriters and computer facilities rather than a pen or pencil. This has created problems in the past because of the extra noise that such machines make in the classroom. Modern technology has certainly helped to cut this down to a large extent and has helped in both the production of high quality presentation and variable large size print for children to read more easily. However, the pace at which they can use the machinery remains problematic for some children. Consideration may be given to them being given extra time to complete work.

Both Chapman and Stone (1988) and Best (1992) have produced excellent publications on the management of those with visual difficulties in the classroom. Best's book in particular is aimed at the child in the mainstream school and is full of practical advice for the teacher. If there are difficulties in this area both books are worth consulting. It is also important that SEN staff in the school should be contacted as they may hold valuable information and have useful advice to offer.

CHAPTER 4

Children with physical difficulties, medical conditions and communication problems

INTRODUCTION

For some children their learning experience will be affected by communication problems, physical difficulties or medical conditions. There are an increasingly large number of these pupils to be found in mainstream schools. In many cases knowledge of the children's condition needs to be gained from parents, medical practitioners and, in some cases, other outside professionals concerned with pupils. The educational implications need to be discussed with the Special Needs Coordinator. It is often very difficult to generalise about these circumstances but a basic knowledge of the disabilities and medical and physical conditions of children in their care is essential to teachers, as is information on their educational implications.

Historically pupils with major physical disabilities and medical problems were not generally catered for in mainstream schools. However since the 1981 Education Act this has changed. It is also the case that far more children with unusual medical conditions are to be found in the mainstream school. It is essential that class teachers are successfully prepared to meet these needs. Teachers need to know what these conditions mean in terms of the children's active participation in the school, their mobility and the arrangements which need to be made to accommodate this, as well as developing strategies to facilitate their learning.

Lansdown (1980) and Halliday (1989) identified a list of more common physical difficulties which included asthma, cerebral palsy, cystic fibrosis, diabetes, epilepsy, muscular dystrophy and hydrocephalus. It is information on the educational implications of these conditions and the development of appropriate teaching strategies which will be the focus for this section of the book. A later section of this chapter will consider the impact of communication and language difficulties.

ASTHMA

Asthma is a common medical condition. Some four per cent of the population are asthmatic to a degree. However a much smaller percentage have severe problems. If this is the case for children in your school they may have periods of absence from school. They are also likely to be unable to participate fully in certain curricular activities. The educational implications are:

● the child may need to catch up on missed work;
● PE and games may be difficult to participate in fully and there may be times when alternative activities have to be found;
● cold or dry weather may be more problematic;
● discussion with parents may be necessary to work out how best physical activities might be undertaken;
● food allergies need to be checked;
● reminders may be necessary about the use of an inhaler.

In the event of an attack the basic rules are:

● stay calm;
● ensure that medication is taken;
● call for a doctor if the attack lasts longer than fifteen minutes after the medication, if the shortness of breath continues, if they are unable to stand up or unable to speak, if they are turning blue or the pulse rate exceeds 120 per minute.

BRITTLE BONE DISEASE

Pupils with brittle bone disease are no more likely to have learning difficulties than the rest of their peer group. They may however have difficulties with participation in games and PE and other physical activities. They may also need:

● time to catch up with, or be taught, work which they have missed after periods of hospitalisation (some children may need work for long spells in hospital);
● aids for mobility;
● aids for writing;
● an extra time allowance for the completion of examinations and assessments;
● clutter removed from the classrooms where they are taught to lessen the risk of falling – some in this group will be anxious about the dangers of falling;
● positive intervention to aid emotional adjustment.

CEREBRAL PALSY

Cerebral palsy is a condition caused by damage to the brain. It has three forms: spasticity (where movement is often stiff and jerky), athetosis (manifested through jerky and irregular movements over the whole body) and ataxia (which produces difficulties with balance and coordination). As far as the education of children with this condition is concerned there are a variety of implications:

● mobility problems – some will be ambulant, others will need the use of a wheelchair;
● fine motor control may be affected – this will depend on the limbs the child is being asked to use;
● some may have problems with speech and articulation – for some, aids to help

them record their work or help with speech will be necessary;

- support and intervention from outside professionals will be very likely, as will long periods of hospitalisation – extra teaching or time to complete work will be necessary when this is the case;
- some will have negative feelings about themselves and a poor self-image – they may need much support to help them with this.

CYSTIC FIBROSIS

Cystic fibrosis is an incurable genetic disorder, which through the secretion of abnormally thick mucus in the lungs and the pancreas results in obstructions or infections of the bronchial tube or in the stomach. For those suffering from this condition, treatment will be required daily. This may include breathing exercises, physiotherapy, courses of antibiotics and a high protein diet to aid digestion.

Children with this condition are no more likely to have learning difficulties than their peers. Any effects on the achievement of children with this condition is likely to have been caused by absence and hospitalisation. With care they should be able to participate fully in the curriculum programme. However, within this certain specific allowances will need to be made. These might include:

- a room with privacy if postural drainage is necessary;
- longer time to eat their meals.

Beyond this they may need to be excused PE on a regular basis. Since they may have a persistent non-infectious cough and regularly feel ill they may need to spend time at home. For some the option of home tuition could be a possibility.

DIABETES

Diabetes is caused through the breakdown of the production of insulin in the body. Children can often develop diabetes suddenly and need insulin and dietary provision to control it. An imbalance of blood sugar in the body will make the child unwell. Too little glucose will result in headaches, paleness, sweating, shaking, confusion, fear or mood swings.

The educational programme for those with diabetes should follow the normal course. The teacher will need to be aware of any of the above symptoms and, if possible, be prepared with extra food for the child to eat in their lessons. In some circumstances the child will be able to recognise when problems are starting and ask permission to eat in class. This should be granted.

School trips will need to be organised carefully to ensure there are opportunities for eating stops. If this is taken into account the child should be able to participate fully in all activities. A useful school pack is available from the British Diabetes Association.

EPILEPSY

Epilepsy is a cerebral disorder which develops suddenly, ceases spontaneously and has a tendency to recur. Usually it needs controlling by drugs. Haskell and

Barrett (1993) indicated that it is a condition which affects up to 18.6 of every thousand people. There are a number of factors which can cause a fit. These include physical illness, emotional and physical strain and the inadequate administration of drugs to control the condition. However, those with this condition can generally successfully attend school without too many difficulties. Often however their condition will lead to underperformance.

There are a variety of types of epilepsy. Tonic clonic seizures (Grand Mal) is the most dramatic, where a child can have a fit, lose consciousness, have body spasms and sometimes lose control of their bowel or bladder. A facial fit will manifest itself in a similar way, except that it may not affect the whole body. Absence seizures (Petit Mal) often appears as a momentarily lapse of attention. As a consequence of petit mal concentration will have been lost and instructions will have to be repeated. Myclonic epilepsy is indicated through brief muscle contractions or distentions in the neck, while akinetic epilepsy is a situation where a child may drop to the floor momentarily and recover. In some circumstances the different types of seizures can combine in one person.

In many cases the life style of the epileptic is no different from that of anyone else. The British Epileptic Association suggests that as few restrictions as possible should be placed on the child. It states that on some occasions rope-climbing activities may be unwise but providing there is supervision there is no need for other restrictions. Swimming usually causes no problems and this should be encouraged with the provision of a lifeguard at the side of the pool.

It is useful to know what actions to take in the event of an attack. The best approach is to:

1. Keep calm yourself and reassure the other children in the room.
2. Loosen the child's clothing in the neck region.
3. Place the child in the semi-prone position, with the head on its side.
4. Look at the child's eyes and facial colour.
5. Check the breathing and the pulse rate.
6. Monitor the length of the attack. If it lasts more than five minutes call a doctor or have the child sent to hospital.

MUSCULAR DYSTROPHY

Muscular dystrophy is a wasting disease which has no known cure. It is a condition which does not affect the brain but does affect motor skills and levels of personal independence.

As the influence of the condition increases it is often necessary to make decisions affecting the location of the child's educational provision. For some there will be increasing difficulties as its effects increase and there may be need of a home tutor; others will need placement in a special school.

The only outcome of the condition is death and the child, their friends and the teacher will need to be prepared for this through counselling. In the mainstream school death is rare as many children with this condition will have left before this is likely. However, a mechanism will need to be in place to meet such an eventuality.

SPINA BIFIDA AND HYDROCEPHALUS

Spina bifida and hydrocephalus are a group of conditions relating to the malfunctioning of the spinal cord. For some the condition is mild and has little effect on their lives; for others however its manifestation is much more serious, leading to permanent damage. Hydrocephalus is caused by pressure on the brain. If it is left untreated it can lead to blindness, brain damage or death.

These conditions can lead to mobility problems. Walking aids and wheelchairs are often required by sufferers. This can lead to limited access to educational and learning opportunities. This difficulty can also be accompanied by difficulties with:

- specific learning problems (some conditions have more manifestations of this than others); intelligence can also be affected by the severity of the hydrocephalus;
- judging size, distance or direction;
- forming concepts;
- fine motor control;
- personal organisation.

With these points in mind it essential that an individual assessment is undertaken so that good planning can be undertaken to meet the needs of the child.

COMMUNICATION AND LANGUAGE DIFFICULTIES

Some pupils with special needs will have difficulties in communicating with other children and their teachers. For those children who have difficulty forming their thoughts or who have speech difficulties this can be a considerable problem. Sometimes these children appear very quiet, shy and uncommunicative. Language and speech are both vital components in the learning process and for those with difficulties in this area there will be consequent problems.

Beyond those with hearing difficulties discussed in Chapter 3 there are a number of other conditions which will impede children's language development. Webster and McConnell (1989) and Martin and Miller (1995) have categorised several types of language delays: global, developmental, language disorders, environmental difficulties and social class difficulties.

Global delay

Global language delay exists when the general level of ability of the child, and not just their language skills, lag behind that expected for their age group. An example of someone who could be placed in this category is a child with Down's syndrome.

Developmental delay

Developmental language delay is related to the area of language and speech development only. Other aspects are not causing concern. An example of this is a child suffering from auditory perceptual difficulties, whose language skills are delayed but who otherwise is developing normally.

Language disorders

Language disorders generally involve delays in both language development and in the language patterns exhibited by the child. Children in this category typically experience considerable difficulties and may need help from speech therapists. Most common among these children are those who are autistic, dyspraxic or aphasic.

Autistic children have major communication problems which can be both immature and deviant. This is often accompanied by bizarre behaviour. The most severe cases of autism will need specialist help, usually organised outside the mainstream school. Dyspraxic children are unable to programme their speech muscles to produce sounds for acceptable speech. Those who are aphasic have problems in understanding spoken language and are unable to use it appropriately. All these disorders result in children experiencing considerable difficulties in learning generally, and in developing literacy skills in particular.

Extra help needs to be provided in the most difficult cases by specialist teachers and therapists, who may work on a one-to-one basis with them. Those with less severe problems in the mainstream school will exhibit difficulties in communication. In question and answer situations in normal lessons they are unlikely to join in even when asked directly by the teacher and may be reluctant to do so even in small group or one-to-one situations.

Environmental difficulties

Environmental language difficulties are manifested in the living conditions of children. In some cases where parental language is limited the children will have similar difficulties. This can also be the case for children where both parents are deaf or where the first language of the home is not English.

Social class difficulties

Conditions relating to social class have also been identified as being related to language development. However, this area is contentious. Bernstein (1970) and Tough (1977) argued that at the pre-school stage pupils from disadvantaged homes were much less likely than middle class children to use language for complex purposes. From this assertion the view emerged that there was a gap between children from different social classes in respect of their language acquisition and development. It has also been argued that cultural differences, particularly in the early years of development, have a marked effect on the performance of a child in school. Factors such as the interaction between mother and child, the language patterns at home, attendance at nursery school and the attitude of the parents to school could, it was suggested, have considerable effects on a child's educational performance.

More recent research, however, indicates that this situation is not so clear cut. Tizard and Hughes (1984) argued that there was a considerable overlap between the language patterns of different social classes and teachers should be aware of this. Nevertheless language acquisition is a major factor in a child's development in so many ways in school, particularly in the development of reading. Therefore considerable attention needs to be given to this area of work. For some children language enrichment programmes may be necessary to aid their development

Facilitating language development

Miller (1996) indicated that many language difficulties will be resolved naturally through the variety of activities provided at home and school. In this respect she advises a policy of professionals working together with parents. Where problems remain Webster and McConnell (1989) argue for a 'naturalistic' approach through the spontaneity of the use of language.

As part of this they advocated an integrated approach with a flexible support system to maintain this approach. Further, they emphasised the importance of classroom management techniques. These are based on good practice to be found in the repertoire of many teachers: gaining the attention of the child, having a sense of purpose, regular and systematic feedback, focusing on and isolating the main features of the tasks, checking instructions and providing positive feedback to the child. This approach is discussed in greater detail in Chapter 8 dealing with classroom management issues.

Miller (1996) also provided an itemised list of helpful tactics for the classroom teacher. The key points are:

- Accurate listening to what the child is saying, when this takes place and how it is done. This she argues is the key strategy.
- Attempt to analyse if the child has difficulties with expressive language or understanding that of others.
- Check the curriculum for its vocabulary, ideas and concepts.
- Consider how the individual child can be helped. Check your own language level against this.
- Where there is a lack of clarity of speech from the child ensure they can indicate when they have understood.

To aid the teacher Webster and McConnell (1989) provided lists of suitable objectives for children and adults who are working with them. These, when accompanied with brief case studies, could prove to be of considerable value to the practising teacher.

There have been a number of other useful publications on approaching speech and language difficulties for the classroom teacher. These include Hutt (1986) and Kersner and Wright (1996) – both provide useful information for those working in the mainstream school.

CHAPTER 5

Practical considerations

INTRODUCTION

This chapter examines some of the practical considerations which may need to be taken into account with pupils with SEN. These include issues relating to curriculum and class management, communication, working with other professionals and classroom helpers, difficulties relating to out of classroom activities, and relationships with other pupils. A number of important factors will be discussed including movement around school, toileting arrangements, out of school activities and relationships with other children.

THE CURRICULUM

In many cases a child with SEN can cope adequately with the curricular programme of the mainstream school. Indeed many pupils with a Statement of Special Educational Need have this as a requirement of provision. Where this is the case, Male and Thompson (1985) argued that a balance must be struck between the special needs of the child and the opportunity for them to participate in the widest possible general school curriculum. Further, they point out that ultimately this must take the form of a compromise based on the individual needs of children. In essence it is more a question of pace and differentiation within the curriculum as well as realistic expectations from the teacher.

DIFFERENTIATION

Differentiation is about correctly matching the work expected from pupils with their ability to do it. It is an important skill which needs to be developed by all successful teachers. Reynolds (1992) indicated that aspects of the skills in differentiation need to be covered at initial teacher training level. Differentiation is a developmental skill which needs much practice to gain consistency. For those working with pupils with SEN, particularly learning difficulties, it is an area of particular importance.

Differentiation can be undertaken in a variety of ways. The skills fall into two major areas: by the tasks set for pupils and by the assessment of the outcomes produced by them. However, for those children with SEN other factors are of importance. These include the pace of the completion of the work by children, the expected level of performance relating to their ability, the resources used and the support provided to help in their achievement.

The nature of many special needs affect children's ability to concentrate on their work to the same extent as the majority of their peers. Problems will occur with the pace of lessons because of factors such as the speed of the work and the tasks demanded from them. This can lead to fatigue and, in some situations, an inability to concentrate for more than a few minutes at a time.

In some circumstances children with SEN may become tired more easily than other pupils, affecting their learning. Tiredness can most easily be observed in the afternoon, and teachers should take this into account in their planning. If possible new learning should be undertaken in the morning. The school timetable can make this difficult and in such circumstances a careful watch may need to be kept on vulnerable children. Tiredness is sometimes difficult to discern, but close observation between pupil performance at different times of the day will be helpful here. It is also generally the case that younger children are more prone to tiredness than older ones.

The importance of correctly addressing the level of ability of children with SEN is the major theme of this book and particular strategies for important aspects of this are important considerations throughout it. For those looking to widen their knowledge on the wider issues of differentiation, Barthorpe and Visser (1991) is a useful starting point.

HOMEWORK

In theory there is no reason why pupils with SEN should not attempt homework in the same way as other members of the class. In practice some will be able to cope with the demands much better than others. The success of this will depend largely on the individual nature of the problem and every case should be judged on its merits.

The question of the organisation and setting of homework is important for children with physical problems. Some children will need to leave lessons early to avoid congestion in the corridors. If the work is to be set it is important this is done before the end of the lesson if the child is to copy it down before they leave.

The question also arises as to the physical fitness of children to do the homework, and the effect such an extra strain may have on their physical well-being. As with the points raised earlier about the tiredness of pupils in class, individual teachers need to use their discretion here.

ADDITIONAL HELP FROM OTHER PROFESSIONALS

The most common forms of additional help needed by pupils with SEN are physiotherapy and speech therapy. In both cases the times for receiving this help will not be set by the teacher, and the child may have to leave lessons at times when it is inconvenient. There is a considerable need for cooperation and flexibility between the various professionals so that the work can be done with the minimum of disruption for all concerned.

The value of liaison with other professionals cannot be overestimated. They will be able to provide a useful insight into the needs of individual children which may not manifest themselves in the classroom situation. In some cases, if they have worked with the child in a previous school, they may be able to detail important background information. This will help to provide a better, more comprehensive picture of the child. Exchanging information and views can also help to identify potential difficulties and promote the development of strategies to accommodate or even avoid these.

Finding time to meet can be difficult, since the professionals can work in several schools during the week. Usually they can be contacted and a meeting can be arranged, even if it can take a little time.

WORKING WITH OTHERS IN THE CLASSROOM

Thomas (1985) described working with others in the classroom as the 'key to integration'. Staff working cooperatively with other colleagues and ancillaries – such as teachers' aides, classroom assistants, non-teaching assistants (NTAs) and special needs assistants (SNAs) – can have a considerable bearing on the rate of development and the successful integration of the pupils for whom it is provided. Further, such cooperation can have an important bearing on the viability of arrangements which have been made.

The role of the teachers' assistant and their professional relationship with the class teacher is vital. The assistant needs to be well informed on a number of aspects of any lesson at which they are present. These include most importantly:

- the content of the lesson and teacher expectations of the children about whom they are concerned;
- the teacher's awareness of potential difficulties of pupils;
- teacher expectations as to the role of the assistant during the lesson.

The teacher is, of course, in overall control of the lesson and its direction and content. In this situation the teacher's role is to design the appropriate learning programmes and that of the assistant to implement it. However, the relationship with the assistant should be conducted on a 'two-way' basis. They have on many occasions useful suggestions to make with regard to children's work and progress, or relevant knowledge of them in another situation which could be influential in future planning.

The question must also be raised as to the overall role of assistants in the classroom. It must be decided whether they should work with other pupils experiencing difficulties as part of their learning process in the class or work only with those designated to them. The evidence of good practice indicates that the teacher must be flexible; with the assistant, although focusing primarily on their designated child for much of their time, also working with others who need help when this is appropriate.

Experience indicates that the rest of the pupils in the class resent one child monopolising the assistant. On the contrary they welcome the extra time which they can be given. Further, if the aide works with the whole of the pupil group it tends to benefit the social integration of the targeted pupil.

MOVEMENT AROUND THE SCHOOL

Some children experience difficulties in getting around school. For some this will relate purely to problems caused by their disability; in other cases these problems will be worsened through the design of the building or perhaps its geographical layout.

In some circumstances it will be necessary on the part of teachers to allow some children to be late for lessons because of a difficulty in getting to the classroom; in other cases it may be necessary for a pupil to leave lessons early to be clear of the rush in the corridors. At certain times specific arrangements may have to be made on behalf of pupils so that they are not late for examinations or tests.

The use of a trolley to help in the movement of a pupil's equipment can be useful. For some children who have difficulty in getting round school, a nurse or aide may be required. This may help in the overall movement of children during the day, and liaison between the teacher and the aide can help all concerned to iron out any problems which may occur.

SPECIAL TOILETING ARRANGEMENTS

A small number of pupils will have difficulties with their toileting arrangements. There are a number of conditions which demand that a child will need to go to the toilet at inappropriate times during a lesson. The difficulties this will cause to the pupil will vary according to the medical problem.

From the teacher's point of view these disruptions are often irksome and are often a source of embarrassment to the pupils themselves. It is best, if at all possible, that a routine for visits to the toilet be worked out. The best times are of course break times and lunch times and if it is at all possible the routine should incorporate this pattern. The routine, however, must not be inflexible and there must be room for latitude in allowing a child who has problems to go to the toilet on request. In certain cases contact with parents may be imperative or even with the medical services.

The key factor to be kept at the forefront of the teachers' minds is the health and well-being of the child in question and his or her social acceptance among peers despite their difficulties.

OUT OF SCHOOL ACTIVITIES

In order to encourage a feeling of full personal integration, pupils with SEN require access to as many out of school activities as is possible. However, in certain situations they may need to be counselled to dissuade them from participating in particular activities. On many occasions they will be able to participate in most things with a little planning by the staff concerned. Some of the factors which need to be taken into consideration include access to the minibus, the need for extra or special medical supplies, extra clothing or food, the need (if relevant) for a wheelchair or folding chair, toilet stops and extra adult support and assistance. A useful guide on planning outdoor activities for the disabled is available (Croucher, 1988).

RELATIONSHIPS WITH OTHER CHILDREN

The success of the school experience for some pupils with special needs can be gauged by their level of acceptance by others. This can be the first and most crucial hurdle. The staff in the school and its organisation can be vital here. The key points, in this respect, can best be raised as questions on specific issues. Some of the more important ones are presented in the following paragraphs.

How is unsupervised time dealt with? Are pupils expected to get on as best they can or are other arrangements made for those with special needs? If other arrangements are made, are pupils who do not have special needs excluded? If they are excluded, what effect does this have on both parties?

Mealtimes can be a traumatic experience for pupils with particular difficulties. If the canteen is self-service, does that produce any problems? Some children have particular dietary restrictions. Are these dealt with in a thoughtful and considered way? How are those on free school meals treated; are they likely to be embarrassed by this?

As discussed earlier, toileting problems still persist for some pupils into the secondary school. In some cases the communal school toilets will not provide sufficient privacy for some pupils, and special arrangements may need to be made. Similarly, special arrangements may be appropriate for some when changing for games or PE. How does the school react to this situation? What solutions has it come up with?

Acceptance of those pupils with special needs is dependent upon the attitude of the whole school to them. One key factor is the rationale used to allocate them to classes. Do all the pupils with special needs in the same year group end up in the same classes all the time? What effect does this have on them and their teachers? Are the other children in the class sympathetic and understanding? Will the pupils with special needs be withdrawn from the normal timetable? If this is done, in what circumstances? Is there a programme specifically designed for some children to help them develop their skills? How is this organised and what costs or benefits are there for these pupils?

CHAPTER 6

Assessing pupils

INTRODUCTION

The process of assessment can take two forms: formative and summative. It is formative assessment which is the focus of this chapter. The process of assessment is complex, based on such factors as the curriculum programme, the needs of the class as a whole and those of the individuals within it. This can best be shown in diagrammatic form as in Figure 2, which presents the key issues in a simple format.

Summative	Formative
Often formal situations	Often informal but not always
Purpose	**Purpose**
To provide an overall view	To check on progress or find specific
Often linked with outside	information
syllabus requirements	
Examples	**Examples**
National Curriculum (SATS)	Informal tests, diagnostic assessments
GCSE, A level	
Records of Achievement (RoA)	

Figure 2 The relationship between formative and summative assessment

Children who are being assessed often are placed under a degree of strain and it is often argued that this is unhelpful in demonstrating their true capabilities. This is difficult to assess reliably but nevertheless it is an important consideration and should be taken into account when children are undertaking assessments.

THE ASSESSMENT FRAMEWORK

Increasingly, assessment of the curricular programme is set in a framework determined by factors outside the immediate control of the classroom teacher. One example of this is where the syllabus is determined by the needs of formal external tests or examinations such as the Standard Assessment Tasks (SATs) taken at the ages of seven, eleven and fourteen, GCSE and A level examinations.

However, information about a pupil's ability can be gained from a number of important sources other than formal examinations and tests that have been conducted. These may include school transfer documents and reports, information obtained by the SENCO from discussions with parents and previous teachers, as well as from screening information obtained on entry to school.

APPROACHING ASSESSMENT

Assessment can initially be divided into two areas: informal and formal. The SATs, when undertaken by pupils at the ages of seven, eleven and fourteen, are formal tests. The National Curriculum Assessment Arrangements (National Curriculum Council, 1989a) described their purpose as helping teachers 'to identify where further diagnostic assessment is necessary'. The *Parent's Charter, Children with Special Needs* (DES, 1994) reiterated this point.

However, this type of assessment is often of little value to the teacher since the time lapse between each test is considerable and the information received unhelpful on a day-to-day basis. Teachers need to know much more detail about the level of skill of the pupils in their class. There are two ways of approaching this. If, for example, it is considered that greater knowledge of the reading skills of pupils would be valuable, a formal diagnostic test may at some stage be appropriate. However, informal testing can also provide valuable information through a quick overview of the pupil's reading levels.

INFORMAL ASSESSMENTS

In order to develop the skills of pupils, teachers must initially be able to identify a starting point for pupils within the class. This in turn must also be part of an organised process. The experienced teacher, working with a new group of pupils, will not only spend time getting to know them but also spend time investigating what they have learned already and also their level of understanding. In this way the teacher is beginning the process of assessing the needs of the pupils and identifying starting points for them.

An example of an informal test might include checking on the reading skills of the class by asking them, in turn, to read from one of the pieces of selected material for that course of study. This will provide some information about the level of material which has been selected.

However, for those children where there is hesitation or apparent difficulty this approach will not be sufficient. It will not tell for example if a child's difficulties are related to a number of crucial factors. Examples of these include:

- anxieties about reading aloud in class (a particularly relevant point where the class is new to the school or to the teacher and the children may have heightened anxiety as a consequence of that);
- if it is a sight problem and children have merely forgotten their glasses;
- children have reading difficulties which need further investigation.

Similar procedures are appropriate for informally assessing the level of skill of pupils in other subject areas. The approaches can vary from subject to subject across the curriculum but most teachers devise ways of doing this in their subject area in order to find a satisfactory starting point for teaching and preparing the differentiated levels of learning material.

TACTICS AND STRATEGIES

A point worth bearing in mind when pupils transfer from one school to another is their experience of copying from the blackboard. Commonly there is much more likelihood of use of the blackboard in the secondary than in the primary school. The skills involved in copying from a piece of written work from the board, although patently simple perhaps to the teacher, may not be so easy for some of the children.

A simple exercise to check these is completing the information on the front of an exercise book, writing down the date and the title of a piece of work or copying down the laboratory or classroom rules. A walk round the classroom to look at what has been produced can be very revealing and can give, at least in outline, a good initial indication of some of the difficulties of certain pupils. This quick overview will not only provide an indication of copying skills but also will provide the teacher with an impression of the writing and close motor control skills of the pupils in their class. At the age of eleven for example a typical mixed ability class will contain children covering the whole range of ability in this area – from those whose writing and presentation is stylish and careful, to those who are having difficulty in forming their letters correctly.

HANDWRITING AND READING DEVELOPMENT

A point must be made in relation to handwriting. It is easy to relate poor handwriting and untidiness with poor ability. This is dangerous in the extreme as some of the brightest children can have a poor handwriting style. It is unproductive to relate the two factors too closely together as well as being grossly unfair on the child.

However, in circumstances where there is a combination of weak reading, poor copying and immature handwriting skills, these may be important signals and should perhaps be regarded as indications that further formal diagnostic work is necessary. It is only when this is completed that any true indication of the level of ability of the child can be made. It is in these circumstances also that further professional advice and experience will be useful. For example it can be very useful to discuss your views with the Special Needs Coordinator or those working in the special needs department. They may have useful information on the child and on appropriate teaching techniques. Further information on teaching handwriting is included in Chapter 10.

In other circumstances, where handwriting is a special difficulty a typewriter may be necessary. In these situations a silent carriage device is essential in the normal working atmosphere of the classroom.

Some children will need adaptations to their writing equipment, such as enlarged hand grips. For some it will be necessary to anchor the paper while they are writing so as to get the best results. Mats which will do this are available through specialist outlets such as the LDA in Wisbech.

FORMAL ASSESSMENT

For some children informal assessments will not provide enough information for the classroom teacher. In such circumstances a formal test (or a series of them) may be valuable. A number of considerations need to be taken into account by teachers when assessing pupils with SEN. These include:

- the specific purpose which they have in mind when thinking about testing a child, or a group of children;
- the variety of tests available for use in school;
- the differences between tests which measure potential and those which measure performance.

Tests of potential often produce an outcome which is given as a quotient. The measurement of intelligence (IQ) is a familiar example of this. These tests measure a child on a given scale against a set of predetermined norms. The tests are therefore referred to as norm-referenced tests. The normal curve of distribution (see Figure 3) is useful in that it illustrates the typical distribution of scores obtained on norm-referenced tests. It is important to stress that there are problems with using this type of assessment with children with SEN. The information they provide is often of little value to the classroom teacher as it is set in comparative terms to other children and has no diagnostic value. To obtain useful information this type of test is best administered by other professionals such as educational psychologists.

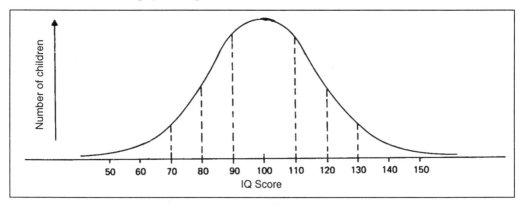

Figure 3 The normal curve of the distribution of intelligence

Alternately, in other types of test, a measure of performance is set against a particular level of skill on a specified task to indicate a level of competence. These are called criterion referenced tests. The National Vocational Qualifications (NVQs) are good examples of this approach, as is the driving test for a motor bike or car; where, provided you perform the tasks correctly, you will pass. In this situation there are no limits on the number of people who can pass the test.

THE PURPOSES OF FORMAL ASSESSMENT

Macintosh and Hale (1976) indicated that there were six major purposes for which formal testing could be used. These were *Diagnosis* – to elicit the problems associated with the learning difficulties of a group of children. *Evaluating*, taking stock of a teaching situation, for which some form of formal testing may be useful. *Grading*, a common use for formal testing when results can either be compared or when grades can be awarded. *Guidance* – using testing to help pupils towards a decision relating to their work or future career. *Selection* – using a test to make a choice about a child or for a child to make a selection for itself, for example as in career selection. *Prediction* – using a test as a forecast of a probable outcome

TYPES OF FORMAL ASSESSMENTS

From the point of view of classroom organisation there are two approaches used for formally assessing children in school: group tests and individual tests. In both cases there is a wide range of material available. For anyone wanting to move into this area publishers' catalogues are a good starting point. The advice of other teachers who have used such material will also be invaluable.

Group tests

Group tests can be conducted with a whole group of pupils at one time. Many are designed to be administered in a set period of time. These tests are usually relatively easy to mark. Examples include the Wide Span Reading Test (Brimer and Gross, 1972), the Gap Reading Comprehension Test (McLeod and Unwin, 1970), the Verbal Reasoning Test (NFER, 1990). These assessments deal essentially with the level of comprehension of children's reading. This is tested through allowing children to read and work with words in sentences or paragraphs. The exercises they have to complete varies with each test. Broadly the more they complete successfully, then the better their level of skill.

This level of skill is often indicated as a reading age detailed in years and months. This works on the premise of the better the reading age achieved by the pupil, the better the level of reading ability. For some teachers this is a useful guide as to the level of skill of the pupil and the appropriate level of work for them. In practice these reading ages are often difficult to work with. (Just how, for example, does an eleven-year-old in Year 7 with a reading age of seven years and six months perform, or what are the implications for the teacher of having a Year 5 child in the class with a reading age of six years.) Often there will be need for interpretation of the information from such assessments. This can generally be obtained from the SENCO.

Individual tests

Individual reading tests are those undertaken with one child only at a time. Some of these tests are concerned solely with word recognition, while others have a wider diagnostic function. Word recognition tests focus only on the ability of children to recognise the words on the card in front of them. In the case of the Burt or the Schonell graded test the cards shown to the pupil contain a list of graded words. These vary from the easiest such as 'am', 'the' or 'milk' to the most complex such as 'somnambulist' and 'idiosyncrasy'. In test conditions children will read through the list until they make a set number of errors. From the number of words which have been read successfully a score can be obtained. These scores are converted into a reading age which can be compared with the child's chronological age.

Although the use of word recognition tests has some value in the assessment of reading, it takes no account of the pupil's ability to understand what has been read. Others such as Neale's Analysis of Reading Ability (Neale, 1958) assess the comprehension skills of readers and provide a more solid body of information for the teacher to work with. The individual nature of this type of test means they are time-consuming to use. In a busy classroom time for this can be difficult to arrange.

For children with a poor reading level the British Picture Vocabulary Scale (Dunn, undated) may be appropriate. This takes two forms – a long and a short version. (The long version undertakes a more detailed assessment than the short version, but takes longer to complete.) This instrument tests children's vocabulary levels and requires no reading ability on the part of those children being tested. Further it is suitable for the complete school age range.

Individual tests with a diagnostic capability

In some cases the information from the reading age alone, however it is collected, will not provide sufficient information for the teacher about the reading difficulties of children in their class. For some children the relationship between their reading and chronological ages may be wide. The thirteen-year-old with a reading age of less than seven, or those who appear to have a weakness in particular aspects of their reading skills, are examples of this. In these cases further investigation may be vital and this may well have to be done on an individual basis. The assessment materials used for this purpose are individual diagnostic tests.

A good example of this type of test is the Aston Index (NFER, 1976). This assessment package provides a detailed profile of information about the strengths and weaknesses of children's underlying reading skills. These include their visual and auditory perception and their sequential memory skills.

As part of the Aston Index profile, there are a number of sub tests. The Schonell word recognition and spelling tests are included in the Aston Index as is the Goodenough Draw a Man Test. The whole package does not have to be completed and some pupils may undertake only the parts which are relevant to their difficulties. However, if the whole test is completed a profile of achievement can be obtained which will indicate not only children's reading strengths but also areas of weakness which need to be developed.

As far as reading is concerned a full diagnostic assessment may include sections on picture recognition, vocabulary skills, tests of eyesight and hearing, and laterality – their use of their left or right hand, eye or ear. Tests of this type provide a profile of information about the strengths and weaknesses of the pupil's skills. The profile details specific information on the background skills which constitute the components of reading.

Tests such as the Aston Index also investigate the sound blending skills of children. This is an important component of reading. Children can learn to read by using different approaches. These include the 'look and say' approach (the whole word approach), the real books approach or the phonic method. Whatever the approach, part of the skills of anyone reading anything is blending the parts of a word to make a whole, and thus sense of the word. For some children difficulties in this area will arise in blending the letters 'c–a–t' to make cat. With others the problems will be in breaking down and then blending the parts of a word such as architect or ineradicable. What a teacher needs to know is the stage of development of a child between these two extremes.

For those with blending skill difficulties, there may be a lack of knowledge of the sounds that the individual letters in the alphabet make. To the vast majority of children this is no problem, for a small minority there is only difficulty and confusion. Further information on this point is provided in Chapter 9 which focuses on the development of reading skills.

There are a wide range of tests available to help assess the strengths of pupils in other areas of the curriculum apart from reading. These include other aspects of English such as comprehension and spelling skills, and Maths, as well as skills in History, Geography and Science, behaviour difficulties and career choice. If you are interested in these areas they are worth investigation. Conversations with other colleagues may be useful, as may be publishers' catalogues.

CHAPTER 7

Curriculum planning

INTRODUCTION

Using an appropriate test will allow the teacher to obtain a baseline of what the child knows. It is from this that the programme of work should be devised. This chapter will discuss some of the issues raised with regard to setting up this programme of work. It will discuss appropriate curriculum approaches for pupils with SEN and the relationship between these and the requirements made by the National Curriculum.

The starting point for a programme of work is particularly pertinent and different subjects of the curriculum often need different approaches. Maths for example needs a strongly sequential approach, in that skills often have to be learned in a particular order. With more able children there is a greater ability to generalise and understand not only what they are taught but also its wider application. The child with learning difficulties may have difficulty with retaining the basic information let alone applying it. Here the learning processes involved need to be broken down into short sequential steps.

Experience indicates that this is not an easy process for either the pupil or the teacher. From the teacher's point of view it is not always easy to break down the steps involved into pieces which are manageable for the child. Further it can be difficult to set the teaching out in the correct order for the child to understand the processes. Understanding for the pupil is more than half of the battle, for once they have got the concept of what the process involves the rest is usually easier. However, a further difficulty is the amount of time which it can take and the frustration involved for pupils and their teachers.

PLANNING AS PART OF THE TEACHING PROCESS

The literature on classroom organisation and management emphasises the importance of planning not only in terms of the development of the skills of the teacher (Cohen and Manion, 1992; Kyriacou, 1991; Mitchell and Koshy, 1993) but also in relation to the assessment policy of the school (DES, 1988, 1989; Solity and Raybould, 1988; Wolfendale, 1993).

Certainly, for most teachers, this skill is developed individually and is unique to them and their experience and expectations. Nevertheless there are common factors involved and models of practice have been developed. A basic model has been described by Mitchell and Koshy (1993) involving a three-point focus, described by them as the *planning–learning–assessing* dynamic. The model is seen as cyclical and progressive with the pupil and the teacher in a partnership together, as outlined in Figure 4.

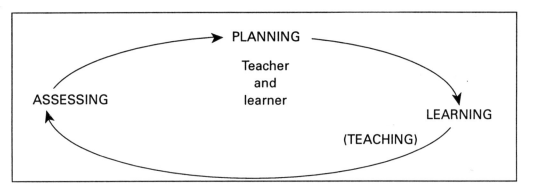

Figure 4 The planning–learning–teaching dynamic described by Mitchell and Koshy (1991)

This model has a definite starting point with the assessment of the pupil coming first. As part of the assessment process the need for evaluation of both what the pupil has done and the effectiveness of the teacher must be taken into consideration. Both aspects are critical to the development of good practice.

However, other key questions for those teachers working with pupils with SEN need to be addressed. The approach outlined in Figure 4, although useful, provides only a skeleton framework. Solity and Raybould (1988) have attempted to fill in some of these gaps. In an approach which they described as 'assessment through teaching' a five-point approach is recommended. This is outlined in Figure 5.

Determining the curriculum sequence
    What skills should I teach?
    In what order should I teach them?
        ↓
Placement on the curriculum sequence
    What does the child know now?
        ↓
Deciding what to teach
    Sequencing
        ↓
Deciding on teaching arrangements
    What methods should I use?
        ↓
Assessing pupil progress
    Evaluating the work done
    How?
    When?

Figure 5 The planning learning and assessment cycle (based on Solity and Raybould, 1988)

The approach presented in Figure 5 is much more detailed and is appropriate for use with children with learning difficulties. It provides a good framework for making teaching decisions. The model is particularly appropriate when the assessment/teaching strategy is being undertaken as part of regular classroom provision, and is seen to be integral to the daily routine of the teacher.

ASSESSING THE PROGRESS OF PUPILS

The question of when to assess the progress of pupils in this way is also an important issue. In broad terms it must be left to the discretion of the individual teacher. In certain circumstances this may have to be done on a daily basis. In other circumstances it may be more appropriate for it to be undertaken at longer intervals. In the normal circumstances in secondary schools this may be necessary because of the way in which the timetable has been organised, whereby the teacher does not see the class every day.

DECIDING PRIORITIES

In many respects the central focus of the curriculum for pupils with SEN will have been determined by the requirements laid down in the National Curriculum documentation. However, for some pupils with SEN the selection of core material, the most fundamental of all knowledge for all pupils, can only deal with the basic requirements of coping and the foundations of independent living in the adult world.

In many respects the fundamentals of the academic curriculum content for children who have the more severe difficulties relate to the ability to read independently and knowledge of basic arithmetic. For some children at school-leaving age these skills will still be a problem and they will have a continuing need for development. The figures nationally suggest that some 10 to 15 per cent of adults can be so defined, a figure which is not unexpected when taken in conjunction with the concept of the 20 per cent of pupils with SEN described in the Warnock Report (DES, 1978) and other similar documentation.

In both primary and secondary schools it is important that the learning diet for this group of children is broad and varied. As with any other pupils, those with learning difficulties need to be stimulated and set a wide variety of tasks to demonstrate their skills and build up their confidence. To concentrate merely on developing reading skills and on the basic four rules of number would be tedious for both the pupils concerned and their teachers. In a very short time such an approach would be self defeating and of little value.

WORKING WITH THE NATIONAL CURRICULUM

The National Curriculum has since the Dearing Review (Dearing, 1993) set the teaching requirements in the main curriculum areas for most of the teaching week. The amount of time which can be spent on activities other than National Curriculum activities varies at each Key Stage; for example Key Stages 1 to 3 allow twenty per cent of timetabled time to be used in this way. *A Curriculum for All* (DES, 1989a) set the requirements of the National Curriculum in the context of every child participating in a broad, balanced and relevant curriculum. Exceptions to this, the documentation implies, will be few and often of a temporary or exceptional nature. Adaptations to the prescribed curriculum beyond this are minimal. The documentation stated this should apply in three circumstances only: for pupils with a particular kind of special need, for pupils whose special needs are likely only to be temporary and individual pupils who are the subject of a Statement under the 1981 Education Act.

The subject orders describe the essential knowledge of each area of the curriculum. For many with special educational needs these are often too difficult and in this sense the teacher is left with the dilemma of deciding what should be regarded as the essential core knowledge for this group of pupils.

The flexibility of this arrangement comes with teachers' freedom to determine their own teaching approaches and the ways of delivering the programme. This is not just the case for pupils with SEN but for the class as a whole. In reality this is a situation which has caused some difficulties and there is evidence to indicate that staff face the dilemma of attempting to accommodate the requirements of the National Curriculum with the level of work of some pupils with SEN in their classes.

With pupils with learning difficulties the problem of poor short-term memory is crucial. It is unrealistic to expect children with this problem to retain information even over a short period of time if no form of support work has been undertaken in the intervening period. In some circumstances children will forget not only the task which was set but that it had been set in the first place! It is important that for these children the reinforcement, often through repetition and over learning, of work done is a key strategy.

LEVELS OF WORK

A major part of the life of classroom teachers is concerned with making decisions regarding the development of learning for their pupils. These decisions are wide ranging but among the most important are the curriculum content and the level of understanding, skill or experience which is regarded as acceptable from a particular child or group of children.

Teachers have to decide the level of work that is acceptable from the groups they teach. Sometimes this will be similar for each pupil. They must all copy down the work from the board, or they must all have reached the end of the questions for homework. In other circumstances the level of acceptable work will vary, with the more able perhaps being expected to produce a certain amount of written work while only a few lines will be acceptable from those who are less capable.

In the first place teachers have to decide what will be the core information that they consider a child should have and what is perhaps more peripheral. In the broad context this decision is implied very strongly through the requirements of the National Curriculum framework. Although of considerable value in an overall sense for most pupils, for pupils with SEN it is not really adequate. For the child with learning difficulties who is finding the work very difficult, the pace of learning expected will be a problem as may be the depth of understanding which is demanded.

A further key decision which teachers have to make is related to the level of understanding which they expect of the children on aspects of the curriculum which they are teaching. This level will vary according to the nature of the child as well as the demands of the teacher.

For those children with SEN the depth of information they can deal with can vary considerably according to their difficulties and also their interest in the subject. This can be a source of considerable frustration for both them and their teachers, particularly where there is a mismatch of expectations.

An area of concern identified by the Curriculum Council (1981) was the issue of differential learning. This was described in some detail by Brennan (1985) who made some important points as far as those pupils with SEN were concerned. His model divided the areas of knowledge and skill into three separate areas. These are shown in a simple form in Figure 6.

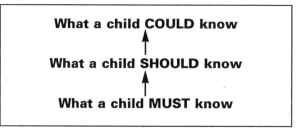

What a child COULD know

↑

What a child SHOULD know

↑

What a child MUST know

Figure 6 Differential learning

In this respect teachers of those with learning difficulties in particular have to select as part of the initial planning for lessons which level to aim for. It has been pointed out in both official documentation and research papers that often the choice of level the teacher makes for this group of pupils is too low for the children they have in mind. Brennan (1985) and others have been at pains to point out the need for teachers to raise their expectations of pupils and to provide them with material and ideas that are both stimulating and challenging for them.

The intention of the Dearing Report (Dearing, 1993) was to allow for a more flexible approach to the content of the curriculum for pupils with SEN and perhaps in turn this will allow for a more realistic approach for the classroom teacher in meeting both the personal and educational needs of pupils.

This model acts only as a guide to the teacher in conjunction with the points made earlier on the National Curriculum documentation on each subject area. To a large extent the subject areas describe the core points for each area of the curriculum. However, experience indicates that for many teachers working with those with special educational needs there are conflicting issues. What for the average and above average pupils can be accepted and assimilated easily as part of their normal learning process can produce considerable difficulties for pupils with learning difficulties.

This was particularly difficult in relation to the original demands of the National Curriculum. The Dearing Report attempted to address, at least in part, some of these difficulties. The intention certainly was to allow for a more flexible approach to curriculum content. It is hoped this will allow for a more realistic approach for the classroom teacher in producing a programme to meet both the personal and educational needs of their pupils.

THE INSTRUCTIONAL HIERARCHY

The idea of the level of instruction is related to the level of difficulty of the task which is set for a child. This can best be explained by remembering that demand for recall of events is easier for a child than those posed in a problem-solving situation, just as asking them to describe an event is an easier task for a child than asking them to explain how or why it happened.

Haring and Eaton (1978) identified five levels of an instructional hierarchy. Strategically the teacher is at liberty to use one or all of these as part of their teaching management skills. This hierarchy is described in simple terms in Figure 7.

The instructional hierarchy

Acquisition
Where pupils are shown something for the first time and learn how to do it accurately

Fluency
When children practice the skill until it becomes second nature to them

Maintenance
When children can perform the skill even when no direct teaching is continuing

Generalisation
When children can use the skill they have been taught in a different context

Adaptation
A situation where children will be set a problem which demands the application of the skill by them independently

---

Figure 7 The instructional hierarchy (based on Haring and Eaton, 1978)

It is within the context of this model that teachers must select their strategy when determining the level of skill required of the pupils in their classes. Factors affecting this choice cannot be solely determined by the views of the teacher but must also bear in mind the level of ability and understanding of children.

DEVELOPMENTAL STAGES OF LEARNING

Piaget described concept formation in terms that were both developmental and which could be linked, in general terms at least, to the mental age of the child. Several schemes have been developed to describe his ideas in simple terms. Perhaps the most popular and accessible is the four stage process outlined in Figure 8.

Stage	Mental Age (approximate)
SENSORY–MOTOR	0–2 years
Pre-operational	(1) **pre-conceptual** 2–4 years (2) **intuitive** 4–7 years
Concrete operations	7–11.5 years
Formal operations	11.5 years upwards

Figure 8 Piaget's stages of development

As far as mainstream schools are concerned most children will arrive at the **Pre-operational** stage. This stage is divided into two distinct parts. The first of these Piaget described as the **pre-conceptual** stage, the second at the **intuitive** level. At this point children's thinking is based on impressions rather than reality. Piaget illustrated this point through the use of a number of experiments related to what he described as conservation. These indicated that children were at a stage where they could not reason reliably, and where sometimes their reasoning would bear little resemblance to reality.

These skills developed at the next level, that of **Concrete operations**. At this stage a child has learned to conserve information to the point where he or she is able to develop reasoning skills to a level where as Child (1993, p.147) puts it 'the child's attention is no longer fixed in one dimension'. Piaget argued that at this level the child would learn sequentially and that for most children this would take the form of a set pattern. This is perhaps best illustrated through examples from maths, where he argues that children learn to conserve ideas about weight before volume since the ability to conserve numbers appears before that of area.

Piaget calculated that only some 15 to 20 per cent of the age group at the time of leaving formal schooling would have arrived at the highest level of thinking – what he described as **Formal operations**. It is a level of thinking that is regarded as being well beyond that of many pupils with SEN in the secondary school and particularly those with learning difficulties. However, this should not be taken as a hard and fast rule for all pupils with SEN. There are pupils with sensory or physical disabilities who are able to operate at the same stage as the rest of their peer group regarding their level of thinking. This is important for the management of learning for any teacher and should not be forgotten.

IMPLICATIONS FOR TEACHERS

The developmental stages detailed above not only help to set the developmental framework for learning and teaching but also help to identify the sequencing skills to be taught. Most pupils, in the primary school and those in their first year of secondary school, will still be working at the concrete operations level of thinking. For those with learning difficulties, as well as a considerable percentage of their slightly more able peer group, this is a level of operation which will not change throughout their secondary schooling.

The most important implications of the views of Piaget for those with learning difficulties can best be summed up as follows.

- In terms of teaching strategies and the ability to learn, the mental age of a child is more important than their chronological age.
- These children, even in the upper school in their GCSE years, need to begin their learning from concrete examples and any conceptual thinking that is required should be introduced slowly.
- Concept formation can only come through the use of the internalisation of the concrete examples used with the pupil. For most pupils with learning difficulties this will be a long-term aim only and may not be achieved during their time at school. A teacher must not expect the impossible nor set their sights too high for children in these circumstances.
- Explanation should accompany experience. The teacher should explain exactly what is required and children need to be helped to understand not only what has been reached in the lesson but how this was done.
- A careful record needs to be kept of the progress of children, so that developments which have been made are clear. This is important for both the pupil and the teacher.
- The use of verbal techniques by the teacher and the interaction between teachers and their pupils is a crucial source of learning for all children. This is accentuated in many pupils with SEN as speech is their main, if not only, source of communication. For some children their skill with spoken language compensates for weaknesses in other areas such as reading or writing.

Each pupil is unique and they will develop learning strategies in different ways from others. An effective learning environment will help them to develop this in relation to their interests and capabilities. Without doubt the more motivated a pupil is the more they will want to learn and as a consequence the more they will learn. There are a number of factors which need to be taken into account in deciding on the possible strategy to employ with pupils with special educational needs.

- Pupils will learn more readily when they are actively engaged in structuring their own programme of work.
- Learning is best undertaken in a holistic way so that pupils will not feel restricted by the subject boundaries. A teacher should be aware of the need to be willing to continuously adjust their expectations to meet this.

- There is the need to take into account evidence which indicates that those teachers and pupils who participate in risk taking in the learning and decision taking process are likely to enhance the pace of learning. It is important that pupils realise that making mistakes is an integral part of the learning process and that they should not be put off by doing so.
- Social interaction fosters ease of learning and opportunities should be structured for various forms of this in classroom activities. There are a number of ways of approaching this with different sizes of groupings and different tasks for different activities. It is worth experimenting here to see which works best with different teaching groups in different situations.

For children with SEN the state of their mind set and their feelings about learning are crucial to their success. This can vary not only from pupil to pupil but also with the same pupil from day to day and therefore great awareness is necessary from the teacher in this area.

TARGET SETTING

Target setting is a vital part of the teacher's role and must be realistic in respect of the ability of children's pace of learning and prior knowledge. In this context accurate feedback on children's work is essential. This is necessary in order to set future targets as well as having an accurate picture of their current point of development.

The management of the curriculum offered to pupils with SEN, particularly those with learning difficulties is vital. It is important that their work is accessible, well planned and prioritised appropriately so they can benefit from their entitlement of a broad, and balanced and relevant programme.

CHAPTER 8

Classroom management

INTRODUCTION

This chapter will focus on the need for good classroom management strategies as an essential part of the role of the teacher. This, it can be argued, is an essential prerequisite for teachers in any situation and for those working with children with SEN this cannot be emphasised too much.

There are various techniques available which the effective teacher is able to draw on and use as the situation demands. Knowledge in this area is acquired through experience and finding out what works best in which circumstances. It is not always easy to understand why one technique, although seemingly appropriate for two similar classes, is much more effective with one than the other.

Factors which may help explain this include the chemistry that exists between the members of the teaching group, the learning style of the pupils and the relationship between the teacher and the pupils. For pupils with SEN, particularly those who have become disillusioned, or disaffected, an awareness of effective classroom management techniques is essential.

TEACHING APPROACHES

Cohen and Manion (1983) outlined six basic approaches to classroom management. These were:

- the **teacher centred** lesson – in which pupils listen to the teacher and the session is conducted as a talk or a lecture;
- **active learning** – where there is discussion and mutual help between the pupils;
- the **lecture discussion** – where although there is lecture format there is interaction between the teacher and the pupils;
- **independent planning** – where the pupils work in small groups and the teacher acts as an 'expert–consultant' among the members of the class;
- **group task centred** – where the topic is the focus of attention and the group work in cooperation with each other as in a seminar situation;
- **independent working** – where the pupils work entirely on their own and there is no interaction between them.

WHAT APPROACHES WORK BEST?

Children with SEN often have problems with concentration. The length of time they are able to concentrate on a task may be relatively short. In this situation it is important that teachers build a range of activities into their lessons. This can take into account not only the problem of the short concentration span but also allow for the development of the whole range of the senses in the programme of work. For some children this is essential to develop the more academic skills as well as bringing variety and change to it.

What is certain is that some approaches with pupils with SEN are more appropriate than others. Of those outlined above the least successful are the teacher-centred and the independent working approaches. Pupils with SEN work best and stay on task longer in a cooperative situation where they have an understanding of the classroom routine and a feeling of some control over the direction of their work.

Beyond this the best approaches rely on a short 'snappy' introduction to a lesson from the teacher and then the setting of tasks for pupils to complete. This approach is not without its problems as during the introduction the class will have to remain quiet, which is not always an easy task for either them or for the teacher. Further, the amount of instructions they can receive will have to be carefully thought out so as not to be so complicated it will confuse them.

The concentration span and short term memories of some children can be surprisingly short. Some will find difficulties in listening beyond the first instruction given to them. With some classes by the time the teacher has said 'come in, take off your coat, sit down' and then followed that by 'take out your exercise book, find something to write with, open your book at the next page and write down the date', some pupils will still be looking for their book and have not listened to any of the instructions which came after that! Careful observation of the class is essential in determining the pace of the instructions given. In these circumstances it is also important that the instructions are clearly understood, and if necessary repeated for those who need it.

DISCUSSIONS

A further useful approach is to engage the class in a question and discussion session. However, this approach can typically only be sustained for about ten minutes of a lesson. An advantage of this approach is that the pupils will have to do no writing, which is a bonus for many of the less able who find this task difficult. However, there are drawbacks to this technique. The first is that the pupils need the ability to listen to each other as well as the teacher, something which can be sorely lacking in some classes. Some children will need training in this skill. To do this in a formal and organised way can be a difficult task. A lot of teacher effort is often needed in setting up this situation if it is to be both interesting and effective.

An important consideration is to encourage participation from as many children as possible in the room. One way of doing this is to work around partially correct answers that are given in the discussion and allow some discussion around what other pupils have said. These partially correct answers can be built up into complete ones. When setting up this situation it is important that the pupils feel comfortable in the situation. Without this there is little chance of them contributing anything.

Further, it is vital that the teacher should be as flexible as possible in the way the situation develops, and allow discussions to incorporate things that the pupils feel are both important to them and that they are comfortable with. It should be remembered that in some cases far more will come from such a situation than could have been expected and those teachers who are prepared to take risks on deviating from their planned lessons can often benefit through the greater participation of pupils. It is important however to retain a sense of balance and to use discretion in such circumstances.

WRITTEN QUESTIONS ON THE BLACKBOARD

A commonly used approach is to produce structured questions for a class either on worksheets or on the blackboard. This can be a useful way to allow the teacher to get around the class to help pupils individually. The best approach is to provide the easiest questions at the beginning. These should be written simply in short sentences and based on concrete examples – perhaps on work provided on the same sheet as the questions or on the blackboard – which the children can do and which will give them confidence. The more open-ended conceptual questions are best left for the later stages of any work to be done. As suggested earlier it is unlikely that those pupils with learning difficulties will get to these. However, with a mixed ability class such an approach will be essential to deal with the needs of the most able. The issues raised here open up the whole question of the preparation and presentation of worksheets. This is a topic which is dealt with in much greater detail later in this chapter.

READING ALOUD TO A CLASS

As mentioned earlier, pupils with learning difficulties work best when there is little writing to be done. Often other activities will appeal to them more as they will not be held back or feel inhibited by their weak writing skills. Many pupils at both primary and secondary level enjoy listening to a story read to them by their teacher, particularly if the teacher is able to read aloud well and is enthusiastic about doing so. Pupils with reading problems can get far more from a story this way than if they have to struggle to read it for themselves.

Using the teacher-led reading aloud technique has benefits in that pupils may decide to volunteer their services to read aloud. It is important not to discourage them to do so. A careful selection of the sentences, a paragraph or a few lines tailored for each child can be useful and lead to enhanced confidence in this skill.

USING THE VIDEO

The question of gaining an insight into a story or play has been considerably enhanced by the video revolution. Most schools have video equipment and it is a useful tool in the teacher's armoury. The visual image can be of enormous benefit to children who are weak academically. It will not only help motivation but also enhance personal internalisation and encourage discussions.

PRACTICAL LESSONS OUTSIDE THE CLASSROOM

Be encouraged to go outside of the classroom to use the school and its environs for practical applications of what you have been trying to teach in school. Properly organised, such experiences can be both valuable and rewarding. Less experienced teachers are often wary of taking a class out of the classroom for fear of difficulties and pupils 'playing up'. The golden rule in this situation is never be 'conned' into doing this by a difficult class looking for an easy lesson. It will not be so for the teacher! Only take them out on your own terms and make it dependent on exemplary behaviour leading up to the trip.

There are a number of activities which lend themselves very well to outdoor activities: survey work, interviews and mapping are some of these, along with a whole host of activities in maths. Work on the local environment of the school can be very useful in that the children will know where they are and be able to talk about it in some detail.

ENCOURAGING THE USE OF DRAMA

Children who have difficulties with reading and writing often enjoy being allowed to act out situations in class. This can be a particularly profitable way of spending time if you are prepared for a certain amount of chaos in the build up and organisation of it. Pupils with SEN often prefer the extemporary approach to drama, when they can put together their own scripts. Their difficulties with role play can be quite marked. Often they find it very difficult to 'think themselves' into the part and they find the empathy that is necessary for this particularly difficult.

Many pupils with reading difficulties prefer reading from a play rather than from a book. The continuous action in the play format appeals to them, as does the short sharp sentence structure of the play as opposed to the more wordy descriptive approach of the novel or reader. They also like to take on the part of the character they are reading. This can be an enjoyable activity for all. Particularly popular are plays that they can see are humorous or relevant to their personal circumstances. There is an increasing amount of suitable material for all age groups available in schools.

WALL DISPLAYS

Children of lower academic ability can gain great benefit from putting together work for a wall display. Pupils with learning difficulties rarely have such opportunities, as the work of others is often chosen as being better or neater. Therefore, having their work mounted on the wall can be a great boost to their confidence.

The cooperative nature of the work appeals to them, as does the strong drawing orientation of the work. One very useful skill that can be introduced in this type of activity is that of tracing from books or other sources. Producing a wall display can often entail a research element and the use of library skills can be included in this activity.

Projects based on the study of local issues often make good topics for wall displays. Not only will this encourage all the skills mentioned above but it will also allow the children to work on a topic which is familiar to them and which may encourage sensible discussion on topics of local interest such as bus routes, planning developments and the siting of local facilities.

The dangers of using the wall display technique are firstly that it can be over-played to the extent that the novelty value wears off. Secondly, in the secondary school in particular, if teachers have a large number of classes it may be difficult to find space to mount all the displays in the classrooms where they teach. This can lead to disappointment and a certain degree of frustration in pupils.

LESS SUCCESSFUL ACTIVITIES

There are a number of approaches and teaching techniques which are generally not successful with the pupils who are academically weak.

Teacher talk. Most pupils in this category will not be able to follow a prolonged talk by a teacher unless the topic is of considerable interest to them and it is done at a pace and with language which is appropriate for their level of ability.

Listening to tapes. A similar point should be made about listening to tape recordings. With very few exceptions the concentration span for this activity is similar to that of listening to teacher talk.

Dictation. In normal circumstances this is a total waste of time for most pupils in this category. They will not be able to take down notes that are read out by the teacher. They will not be able to spell the words required. Copying down at dictation speed is a nightmare for them and also for teachers who will spend their time repeating words or phrases that the children have missed. The approach is often a recipe for disaster.

Taking notes. A similar point needs to be made about taking notes from books. Even bright teenagers in their last years at school find it difficult to pick out the pertinent points from a textbook. For pupils with learning difficulties these difficulties become insuperable.

Unstructured written work. This too is a recipe for disaster as children who have difficulty in writing things down will have difficulty also in coordinating their thoughts on paper. Children in this category will have difficulty in writing a paragraph, let alone an essay!

Fieldwork notes. Writing up fieldwork notes is another task that can only be done within a structured framework devised and closely supervised by the teacher. Without this chaos reigns and the level of frustration can be considerable for all concerned.

If some major piece of writing is required the Cloze procedure is the best approach, where some words are missed out. Even using this approach is not foolproof and the missed out words may have to be written down for pupils to see. Even then the correct word for each blank may have to be pointed out to some individuals.

RECORDING PUPIL PROGRESS

The National Curriculum demands that a record of the work and progress of pupils is kept and varied formats for doing this have been developed in schools throughout the country. These have included written records, tick boxes, the use of charts by pupils or pie charts or graphs. However, records for those with SEN have been part of good classroom practice for many years. Many staff have developed a personal format for their own and the pupils' benefit. They then marry their records with the format demanded by the rest of the school to match the National Curriculum regulations.

A wide variety of possible approaches to this have been identified. This is because of the need to meet a large range of individual circumstances. However, analysis indicates that the formats used can be put into three distinct categories: those kept solely by the teacher, those where the pupils have a role in recording their own progress under teacher supervision and those where progress is indicated through the use of check-lists produced as part of a commercial publisher's scheme.

Records should be straightforward to keep and simple to access. Brennan (1985) indicated that essentially they should be individual, indicate progress and be signed and dated. He suggested further that the information detailed should show:

- the child's relevant problem areas;
- a record of attendance;
- progress – they should have categories of response to indicate the date the work was started and when revision was undertaken;
- the dates when reviews were conducted and their results;
- a place to enter the results of standardised tests and SATs results.

The danger with record cards is their inaccessibility to vital information for all staff. In some schools in order to avoid this problem the record cards of children with SEN are photocopied and distributed to all those who teach them. As part of the responsibilities of the SENCO (or the SEN department in larger schools) the learning, and therefore the teaching implications, are also detailed briefly. Despite the onerous task for those undertaking this, many staff find this a useful strategy. It provides them with valuable information and helps to focus their teaching strategies for these children.

BEHAVIOURAL DIFFICULTIES

It is an increasing aspect of both primary and secondary schools that less motivated and academically less capable children will provide the teacher with more challenging behaviour than some of their more able counterparts. This is more often emphasised when pupils with potential for poor behaviour are placed together for lessons when streaming or setting are used in a school.

Coping with unacceptable behaviour can provide real problems for the teacher, particularly the inexperienced members of staff or those who are new to the school. Without control of the class by the teacher then little or no teaching or learning can take place and chaos will be the result. Evidence from McManus (1989), Ayers, Clarke and Murray (1995) and McNamara and Moreton (1995) indicate that there are both avoidance strategies and modes of effective control which need to be considered by the teacher.

AVOIDANCE SKILLS

There are a number of pointers which may be helpful in working with children who are difficult. These can only act as guidelines as both the situations and the personalities involved will be unique in each teaching situation.

- Expect children to make mistakes and use a teaching model which will take this into account. Children need the freedom to make certain mistakes in an environment which can allow them to correct their errors without fear of condemnation. Many pupils can see the effect of their mistakes and the social consequences of them for themselves and others around them. Explanation in such circumstances can be better than recrimination.
- Have a sliding scale of strategies for discipline. Some children will respond better to certain approaches than others. Some will reach a level of understanding of the consequences of their behaviour before others, even though they may be the same age.
- Be decisive if a child openly defies you. If you allow them to get away with it this will not only show them that they can but give a lead to others of a similar attitude to try their luck. In situations where this happens it is often best to talk to the child away from the rest of the class, so that you are not in danger of drawing comment from them as well. This can only complicate matters, often to your own detriment. It is often useful to make your comments in front of another, more experienced teacher as this lends weight to the situation.

When necessary it can be useful to have a set arrangement which is known by all the class. The use of a red card system to call for assistance from other staff is one commonly used example. Help can be summoned by sending a child out of class to a delegated member of staff with the name of the offending pupil written on it. An awareness of this routine can also help to dissuade others following the offender.

Do not get personally offended by the behaviour. In many cases it is the authority which you represent rather than you as a person which they are attacking. All classes 'try out' a new teacher to see how far they can go and this is a common experience of teaching. To be detached in this situation can be hard, but to deal with a situation in a dispassionate way will be of much greater benefit in the long run. If a child, or even worse a group of children, can see that they can 'get you going' this will only give them encouragement for the future.

Get to know the names of the pupils as quickly as possible. A comment or question aimed at a particular child by name will be much more effective than a general point. In a situation where you are not sure of what is happening, a question to one of those you think is involved will lead to a direct (if often negative response) from that person, as opposed to a question aimed in a general direction only. The general question will alert the offending group of your awareness and in some situations that will be enough. Often you will have to do a follow up question which should be aimed at an individual.

Separate immediately those who are causing you difficulty. You may have to physically reorganise the furniture in the room to do this. However the effort is worth it. Classrooms in the secondary school can be set out in a variety of different ways. The most formal is where they are set out in rows. From a discipline point of view this is the easiest way of keeping order since you can see every face. In some situations where the classroom is not your own or it is a laboratory or practical area where moving the furniture is impossible, it is important that you have the faces of the chief troublemakers sitting towards you, often at the front of the room or even isolated (e.g. under the blackboard) away from the rest of their friends.

Try not to get angry. If you shout, the class will often enjoy the situation even more. Use shouting and anger, acted or otherwise, for key situations. Then it can be really effective. To act out anger is a real and vital skill and very effective with a class without your emotions being reduced to tatters.

Set standards and stick to them. Set them in conjunction with the standards set throughout the school and the school rules. To allow a child to wear an outdoor coat in class, in other than abnormal circumstances, in a school where this is not acceptable can only produce difficulties for you. Similar points can be made about chewing gum, swearing, writing on the covers of textbooks and even seemingly small points like standing up at the beginning or end of lessons.

Be consistent and persistent. Expect the same behaviour from pupils in your class as is the general norm throughout the school. They will be expected to conform elsewhere in the school. Ensure you get the minimum standard at least. However, be realistic in your demands. You cannot expect to get the impossible. Older long-term members of staff will guide you in this respect – ask them if you are not sure.

Don't have victims and favourites. Don't let one child get away with something you have punished another for. This can only cause resentment and a sense of injustice.

Try to solve the class discipline problems yourself in the first instance. There will be times for a number of reasons when this is impossible and you will have to seek the help of others. Children respect you more for dealing with problems yourself. In the eyes of those not involved in the difficulty your ability to deal with the offenders is an additional plus. When a matter is something you regard as serious, tell a more senior member of staff – the head of department or year head. Do not be afraid to do so, particularly if you have dealt with it. It is a good idea to tell the child that you will report a matter to another teacher. This not only indicates your thoughts on its seriousness but also keeps the pupil in the picture – a useful aid in helping to develop a positive relationship with them.

Discuss problem children with other staff. Their experiences with them may help to shed light on the pupil's difficulties and the conversation may also indicate that you are not the only one having trouble with a particular pupil.

Admit the problem exists. Without this as the very first step you can solve nothing.

Enjoy it! Be relaxed with your classes and they will also relax if you give them chance to do so. In general circumstances they appreciate a gentler, good humoured approach rather than a hard and inflexible attitude. It is often easy to observe those who have the potential for trouble. In these circumstances concentrate on the positive and persuasive rather than the inflexible and Draconian.

EFFECTIVE CONTROL

Evidence from McManus (1989), Cohen and Manion (1992) and Kyriacou (1991) indicate that effective classroom control is typically a difficult area for teachers. What teachers feel may be an effective deterrent to pupils is not always seen by them to be so. The evidence indicates that there are three key possibilities which are employed by teachers in school.

Verbal reprimands. Verbal reprimands can be effective if not used too frequently. Overuse can lead to the wishes of the teacher being at best ignored and at worst reinforcing the undesirable behaviour. Where verbal reprimands are used they are best if they are brief, specific to the behaviour, stern, and coupled with some idea for the child as to the required behaviour. Quiet reprimands are far more effective than loud ones.

Detention and lines. Detentions and lines are used frequently by staff and although apparently successful with some children for many they are ineffective. Detentions are the more effective of the two, generally because they ensure the loss of valued free time. They are effective also because on many occasions, for an official detention, the child's parents have to be informed. Some parents will not allow children to be kept in after school hours. This can be an added difficulty and the way round it for the teacher is to keep the child in at break and lunch times for the required time. This is an added burden for the teacher but is often a necessary and useful deterrent.

Contacting parents. Wheldall (1991) indicated that children interviewed indicated that this was the most effective form of punishment. However, this can have problems for teachers who may be new to the school and have had little personal contact with any parent, where the parents are not supportive of the school or where the behaviour persists. In these cases a chat with the head of department or the year tutor can be very effective and may take the heat out of the situation. Contact with either of these people can also act as a deterrent to the future misbehaviour of the child.

Generally, disciplinary measures are more effective when they are:

• immediate;
• built upon good relationship between pupil and the teacher;
• consistent, systematic and predictable;
• not positively reinforcing the undesired behaviour;
• accompanied by clear indications of the desired behaviour.

Work by Wheldall and Merrett (1991) and McManus (1989) indicates that the best approach to class control is through a reward system that underscores good behaviour and work. This results in better behaviour and is seen as the correct approach by the vast majority of pupils. Children view a reward system which involves their parents' knowledge of their progress as being the best approach. The evidence indicates that they prefer time when they have a choice of activities. In the primary school in particular, a choice of the lessons they preferred was seen by pupils as rewards for good behaviour. Rewards are likely to be far more effective where they can be seen by their children to have been earned.

The development of classroom management skills is an important facet of working with children with SEN. Many of them find the process of schooling difficult. Those with learning difficulties in particular often see themselves as failures and become disenchanted and difficult. A positive attitude to their problems by their teachers is essential, as are knowledge and skills in developing suitable and appropriate programmes of work for them.

CHAPTER 9

Developing reading skills

INTRODUCTION

This chapter will concentrate particularly on the development of reading skills for those pupils who find this a considerable problem. Firstly some indication will be given to aid staff in identifying weak readers. The four basic developmental stages of reading will be outlined and issues will be raised with regard to the adaptation and differentiation of teaching materials. Some strategies will also be outlined relating to those pupils with dyslexia.

Any teacher of pupils with SEN will inevitably come into contact with pupils who are weak readers, or even those who have virtually no reading skills at all. This can be a major problem for any teacher from those who have considerable experience to those who are new to the profession. For many pupils described as having special educational needs in mainstream schools poor reading skills will be the crux of their difficulties. This chapter will concentrate on discussing some of the problems which can arise in this area and outlining possible strategies for teachers.

RECOGNISING WEAK READERS

There are certain tell-tale signs that can help a teacher determine if pupils have difficulties with reading (and following from this, the allied skills of writing and spelling). These signs commonly include:

- letter confusion (particularly b, d, p);
- reversals (e.g. 'was' for 'saw');
- difficulties in keeping pace with the rest of the class;
- a tendency to go from right to left rather than from left to right across the page;
- a failure of memory (particularly short term memory);
- failure to use punctuation properly in what is read;
- an inability to build up unknown words by using the sound of the letters;
- an inability to use contextual cues and clues in reading to make sense of it;
- failure to make sense of phrases and sentences;
- poor speech patterns.

Reading difficulties can start with children having problems recognising the names and sounds of the letters in the alphabet. Many capital and small letters in our alphabet are visually very different (e.g. h and H or g and G). For some pupils, for whom visual discrimination is a problem, this can create a major learning difficulty and may take many months or even years to sort out sufficiently for them to learn to read.

This is a situation which is further compounded when the individual letter sounds are combined into groups of two or three. Letter combinations like these make 108 different and recognisable sounds in the English language. Some of the combinations make accessible sounds while others are not used as part of our speech and writing. Examples of this include 'bl' (as in black) or 'sch' (as in school) while 'tj' or 'fw' are not to be found together in normal English usage. It is the problems of the English language such as these that pupils with SEN find difficult to recognise.

THE STAGES OF READING DEVELOPMENT

Reading skills are developmental and as part of the process of learning to read three elements need to be addressed. These are word attack skills, fluency and comprehension skills. Children, as their reading develops, pass through several stages. These stages can in the simplest of terms be equated with reading ages. This is a concept discussed earlier, which gives some indication of the level of reading ability of children and is often used in comparison with the chronological age of the child. Thus a child with a reading age of nine and a similar chronological age will be at an average level in reading skills for this age. Children who are eleven and a half years old, and who have a reading age of eight years, would not only be well below the expectancy for the age group but also would need extra help to develop their reading skills to a level where they could cope adequately with the work with which they will be presented.

Pumfrey (1991), Reason and Boote (1994) and Westwood (1993) indicated there are various stages of competent reading development. Essentially these can be detailed in a four stage hierarchical model.

Stage One (Reading Age less than about seven and a half years)
At this stage the child is still mastering the most frequently used words which make up the language. Examples of these are provided in the Dolch Word List (1954) and the Murray McNally List (1971). Children who are still at this stage of development in the upper primary and secondary school age group will have a poor vocabulary, have considerable difficulties in remembering what has been taught to them and will need constant revision and reinforcement of work which has been done with them. At this stage children will have few or no phonic skills and will probably have learnt words which they can read by sight.

Stage Two (Reading Age about seven and a half to nine and a half years)
This stage of development occurs when children begin to learn the rudimentary aspects of phonics (the sounds which make up most reading). As outlined earlier there are 108 letter combinations which form the recognisable sounds of the language. Some are two letter combinations such as 'sh' or 'th', while others are three or four letter digraphs such as 'ould'. During this stage children will start to develop the skills necessary to recognise some of these

sounds while work will continue to be needed to develop skills and knowledge of the others. At this stage, for those children with difficulties in this area, constant revision and practice will be needed.

Stage Three (Reading Age about nine and a half to eleven and a half years)
It is at this stage that the more complex sounds are being mastered. It is also at this stage that a child will begin to breakdown the sound combinations in longer words to make them more manageable to read. This is a very important developmental skill and work at this level of operation needs to concentrate on the meaning of words and the development of vocabulary as well as the reading skills.

Stage Four (Reading Age about eleven and a half years upwards)
At this stage all the fundamental work on the constituent parts of reading development are in place and children will have the necessary skills to tackle most of the words in the language. By this time difficulties in reading will be dependant on the knowledge of vocabulary and the interpretation of contextual meaning as much as anything else. Children at this stage of their reading development will usually receive help in their normal English lessons.

There is a considerable literature on the teaching of reading available from which further information on a variety of aspects can be gained. Pumfrey (1991) provides not only useful ideas on tasks for developing skills but also some background information on the neurological issues involved. For children at Key Stage 2, Reason and Boote (1994) and Moore and Wade (1995) offer a wide range of strategies for working with pupils who are experiencing difficulties in mainstream schools, while Westwood (1993) provided useful strategies specifically for children with SEN.

HELPING CHILDREN WITH READING

Increasingly as pupils move through school their ability to read will develop. There is so much diversity of progress that by the time children reach the secondary school there is likely to be pupils across the complete range of reading stages in a mixed ability class. Some of these will need only time spent with them and for someone to hear them read in order to alleviate their problems, while others will need long-term help.

These are some activities which may be used at each of the first three stages detailed above. Some of them are more appropriate for individual or small group situations as opposed to a large class environment. It is best to experiment and see what works best for you.

Stage One

- Teach the child the letters of the alphabet; both the names of the letters and the individual sounds they make. In the light of comments made earlier, check on those known and concentrate on a system which includes reinforcement and repetition to ensure knowledge and progress. Use flash cards where necessary. Watch out for 'pitfall letters': those that look alike – a kinaesthetic approach may be helpful here.

- Get the children to trace round dotted letters or simple words.
- Use basic word lists. As with the letters of the alphabet, ensure constant revision and check knowledge.
- Produce flash cards to aid memory and use as a game with rewards for good work.
- Fill in missing letters or phonic sounds in words or sentences. Concentrate on letters or phonic sounds being taught.
- Answer simple questions from a passage of writing to check understanding. Use these for discussion.
- Underline words in a passage of writing.
- Point to particular words or sounds in a selection.
- Look for sounds at the beginning of a word. Play games like 'I spy'.
- Look for similarities in sounds and words. Do work on rhymes.
- Write down what the child says and make a booklet from it. Use illustrations from magazines or books to ensure it is about a topic of their choice. Get the student to read back what you have written.
- Use letter or word bingo with small rewards or prizes.
- Play hangman.

Stage Two

- Use colour to highlight the particular sound or sounds being worked on.
- Work on basic sounds. Cover all 108 sounds to ensure they are known and remembered.
- Dictation of short sentences of a specific sound (no more than five or six words).
- Use jumbled words or jumbled sentences to be rearranged by the pupils. Give lots of help here, some pupils find this exercise very hard.
- Adding an end to a sentence. Keep the number of words required short and simple.
- Comprehension exercises. Produce work cards for the pupils, use on topics of interest.
- Try simple spellings. Use words that are known to the pupil (e.g. those in basic vocabulary lists).
- Use the alternative word approach (e.g.: The fate/fat man was on the bus).
- Put circles around correct sounds in a passage of reading.
- Select correct spellings from a list of alternatives.
- Use punctuation exercises.
- Use of simple crosswords.
- Matching words or matching sound exercises.
- Answering questions on a topical event.
- Reading for interest. Try shared reading among a group of children or perhaps a paired reading scheme with better readers in the class or in the school.

Stage Three

- Use colour to highlight the particular sound or sounds you are working from.
- Match words in sentences and passages.
- Comprehension questions. Use the full range of question types, to encourage deductive skills.
- Work on form filling and letters of application. This is particularly useful with older pupils in their last years at school.
- Break down longer words, e.g. 'em ploy ment' or 'hes it ant'.
- Cloze procedure exercises.
- Spelling exercises to build up known words. Use patterns where words are similar to build on.
- Use of dictionaries to look up words and check spellings.
- Questions on things read from all sources of reading. Use items of interest to the child.
- Reading together; short plays with a small number of parts, or short stories.
- Develop punctuation skills. Concentrate on the basics – full stops, capital letters, sentences.
- Work on elementary grammar; nouns and verbs in particular.

DYSLEXIA

Dyslexia is a specific learning difficulty which affects approximately four per cent of children to some degree. Its cause remains largely unknown, but it can have a major impact on the literacy skills of these pupils. Areas of school work which can be effected include reading, spelling, written work and arithmetic skills. In some cases difficulties in these areas persist, despite normal teaching, and they are seemingly unconnected to socio-economic, cultural or intellectual factors. As a condition it is more easily detectable in pupils with average or above average ability because of the wider gap between their level of intelligence and their abilities in other situations, compared with the level of their literacy skills.

If you consider there are children who may fit the general description of dyslexia check with the school SENCO to see what, if any thing, is already known about them. Most dyslexics, especially those with severe difficulties, need specialist help in small groups. It is unlikely that most staff will have either the time or the expertise to provide such help. However, there are a number of points that the class teacher can help with.

- Allowing a dyslexic child to sit at the front of the class so that observation of the work done and any help required is easy to provide.
- Constant over learning in connection with written language to reinforce points made. A dyslexic child easily forgets in this area of their work.
- Writing clearly on the blackboard and checking that the child has written work down correctly. Part of the problem is that dyslexic children confuse letters and words so that, for example, a 9 may appear as a 6, or p as b.
- Showing patience as children lose their way around school. For the dyslexic

PTO

the sense of time and direction are not good.
- Not expecting them to use a dictionary properly.
- Not expecting reading and spelling skills to improve at the same time.
- Writing out spelling corrections correctly and then allowing time for the recognition of the tricky parts. Writing out the word several times is an appropriate exercise as is the look–cover–write–check procedure outlined in the chapter on developing spelling skills.
- Not providing lists of mixed spellings to learn and test. Spellings are best approached through family patterns of similar sounds.
- Asking children to repeat back what they have to do.
- Listing useful subject words at the back of an exercise book.
- Providing extra time for assignments to be completed.

ADAPTING TEACHING MATERIALS

Adapting material for the less able in the class is an important form of differentiation for pupils. This particularly lends itself to differentiation by the tasks set for different pupils as well as by outcome through the way the different tasks might be assessed. To do this with skill there are a number of important factors to be taken into account. The most important of these is the readability level that the child can cope with. This can be found out through the use of readability tests which are available and can be linked to the school computer. Some of these are complex in explanation and a handbook or the expertise of another member of staff can be invaluable here. A second, and more usual approach, is based on trial and error by the teacher. Here the basic questions are:

- Can the children read it?
- Can they understand it?
- Is it interesting?
- Can they work from it?

Beyond this a number of other points about the adaptation of teaching materials are worth consideration.

Preliminary considerations

- Is the worksheet one of a series of multi-level sheets to be used with a mixed ability group? Is it to be used independently or with small groups? What is the range of ability of the users and how can this be catered for in relation to the content, presentation and readability of both the sheet and the tasks that are set?
- Is the worksheet aimed at promoting enquiry, testing previously taught information, practising skills or other aims? Take into account the need to consider any combination of the aims suggested above, this will have an impact on presentation.
- Is a worksheet the best way of carrying out the tasks? Consider some of the alternative approaches: the use of the blackboard, overhead projection sheets

(if they are simple and clear), cassette recordings or class or whole group lessons. Which approach will be the simplest and most effective? Can any of these be used in conjunction with a worksheet?

- How much will a worksheet cost? How many copies will be required? Will it be reusable?
- Is the worksheet to be evaluated and revised, if necessary? How will this be done? Is this the correct approach? How difficult will any changes be to make? Is there room for an input from the pupils? Their judgement can be of great value.

Writing and design

There are a number of points in the area of the writing and design of worksheets which must be considered.

- The language content must be appropriate for the target group. Look at the words you have used. Are they consistent with the most used and most easily read in the language? How long are the sentences? (in this respect the shorter the better). Are the sentences too complex? (the best approach is one idea per sentence only, with no subordinate clauses). What technical vocabulary must I use, what can I do to make it simpler?
- Beware of over complex or unknown vocabulary, over complex sentences, too large blocks of print, the over use of capital letters, the extended use of personal pronouns and columns of print which are too complex for the children to deal with. The essential message is keep it simple.
- Look at the amount of information on each sheet. Is there too much? Would it be better if there were more than one worksheet to cover the information to be given? Don't make it too long.
- Are the instructions clear and precise? Do the pupils understand the terms I have used? Could I make them simpler?
- Are the drawings or diagrams simple for the pupils to follow? If photographs have been used, do they come out clearly on the copies for the pupils; if they have not, should they be used or would they be best left out?
- Consider the layout and the positioning of the questions or tasks involved. Where is the best place for them in the text? Basically there are four positions: at the beginning of the text, at the end of it, in the middle or throughout it. Select whichever position serves the needs of the children most appropriately.

It is important to explain to the group the aims of the worksheet. This may help them overall and give them some idea of what is being expected of them.

- Match the ability of the pupils and their interests to the tasks they are required to do. Consider the appropriateness of the tasks in relation to the work they can produce and the level of skill and motivation they have.
- Look at the number of tasks they are required to do and the variety of skills they will be faced with. These tasks can include comprehension questions of both the factual or inferential types. (In the light of the overall ability of the

pupils it is an important balance between these, with the accent for the less capable being on the factual/recall format).
- Other tasks can be multiple choice or Cloze type questions, illustrations, labelling diagrams, summaries in either words or pictures, one word or short phrase completion answers or developing or discussing points through small group discussions.
- Do allow enough space for the pupils to write (or draw) their answers. A cramped worksheet can be a very unrewarding experience for any child. It is important to remember that often the writing of those pupils with special needs can be larger than some of the rest of their peer group.

Production

Consider the best type of reproduction and features that are available in the light of the following.
- The general appearance of the document.
- The spacing of the information on the page.
- Breaking up the text with headings or titles to aid the weaker reader.
- The size of the print (remember in particular the needs of those with poor sight). It is also important to look at variations on the size of the print. This will make reading the text more interesting for the pupils and also help to emphasise the more important parts of the sheet.
- The use of coloured paper to coordinate worksheets of a similar theme or on a similar topic. Think also about the use of coloured pens to emphasise points.
- Underlining key words or phrases to emphasise their importance.
- Numbering paragraphs or lines in the text to help those with reading difficulties to find the answers easily.
- If the worksheet is handwritten, is the text legible and is the prose style both easy to read and clear in intent to the pupil.
- Try printing it broadways so that folded it will fit into an exercise book more easily. In this respect ensure the sheets are stuck into the exercise books or placed into folders when completed. Without this they will fall out of the books and get lost.

Presentation

Consider reading the worksheet out aloud for the class. This will certainly help the weaker readers as well as perhaps motivate some of the pupils. Think about presenting the worksheet to some pupils by means of a tape recorder which they can control themselves and allow a degree of independent learning. A further useful idea is to talk about any unfamiliar words or phrases before setting the children the piece of work. As mentioned above, highlight these words as a further prompt in the worksheet.

CHAPTER 10

The development of spelling and handwriting skills

INTRODUCTION

Reason and Boote (1994) argued that handwriting can be effectively used to support spelling with children with SEN. Bearing this in mind the development of spelling and handwriting will be taken together in this chapter.

SPELLING

Spelling is regarded with great importance in society. A high value is placed on the ability to spell by certain elements of society; particularly employers who often associate poor spelling with carelessness. Good spelling has high status in school and is seen as a key factor in discriminating between the levels of skills held by pupils. In this respect it tends to be seen as a characteristic rather than a set of skills which can be learned.

For those pupils who have learning difficulties their spelling can be placed on a continuum from non-existent to having some difficulties with particular words. However, it can be a source of considerable anguish and concern. It is the intention in this chapter to consider the best approach to teaching spelling skills. This will concentrate particularly on the work done by a number of experts in this area (Peters, 1985; Peters and Cripps, 1983; Mushinski Fulk and Stormont Spurgin, 1995a, 1995b; Reason and Boote, 1994).

Some children seemingly have no difficulties with spelling, while others have considerable problems. There is not a strong relationship between the ability to spell and general intelligence, nor is there always a clear relationship between spelling and the ability to read. Some good readers find that they are significantly weaker at spelling. However, as there is a close link between spelling skills and phonic knowledge, it is not likely that a weak reader will be good at spelling. In that sense at least there is a clear connection.

The evidence indicates that as with so many other skills admired and encouraged by the school, good spelling can be related to home background. This Peters (1985) indicated is certainly the case with children up to the age of nine. Cripps (1983) pointed out that better spellers have home environments where they hear conversations, have stories read to them, are good at games which encourage discrimination, have a good visual memory, are able to write quickly and neatly, where their letter formation is accurate, and use a continuous script.

Perhaps surprisingly, evidence collected indicates that the errors that pupils make are generally in only one part of the word, usually in the middle or at the end of it, and these errors often involve only one incorrect letter in the word. In an analysis reported by Peters (1985) it was ascertained that in a group of underachieving children aged nine to eleven some 46 per cent of errors could be related to the confusion and substitutions of letters. Some 23 per cent related to letter omissions and 13 per cent to the transposition of letters. As with reading difficulties, the evidence indicates that spelling errors are often based on incorrect speech habits.

WHY SPELLING IS SO DIFFICULT FOR SOME PUPILS

Peters (1985) indicated that there were four reasons for poor spelling.

- Good spellers have a good internalised spelling system. This can be compared with a musician who can play from memory. This is a facility which is of great benefit to those who have it but is not a gift that all of us have.
- Spelling difficulties are compounded by the tendency of schools and society at large to overemphasise its importance in written work and to take little or no account of the real situation of those who do not have a good internalisation system.
- Children are too often asked to write when the circumstances are not purposeful and because of this there is little need for them to produce writing with a high degree of legibility and correctness in order to communicate with others.
- Spelling is made more difficult by the way it is taught. Despite what we may expect, learning to spell is not the same as learning to read. Whereas some 80 per cent of sounds in learning to read are regular and provide little difficulty for the majority of pupils, spelling difficulties will occur with some of those words because of the different sound patterns within them.

HELPING WEAKER PUPILS

Mushinski-Fulk and Stormont-Spurgin (1995a) advocated an interventionist policy for pupils with SEN. Undertaking such an approach, and bearing in mind the recommended time of one hour to one and a quarter hours each week for instruction (Pressley *et al.*, 1990), their research indicated that such an approach led to an improvement rate of over 90 per cent.

In a survey of appropriate techniques Mushinski-Fulk and Stormont-Spurgin (1995b) identified a variety of approaches to the development of spelling for pupils with learning difficulties. An analysis of these shows that some are teacher directed while others have a more student study focus. These approaches are discussed here in some detail.

Among the teacher focused activities is the 'test–teach–test' approach. This is based on each session on spelling with children starting with a pre-test of the words to be worked with. The lesson focuses on those spelt wrongly at this point, with a final test to check on the progress made at the end of the session. In this way the lesson focuses only on the words spelt incorrectly at the beginning of the lesson.

Peters (1985) and Reason and Boote (1994) have argued that spelling should be allied to grammar, in that it is a form of communication which is concerned primarily with sequencing permissible combinations of words. Spelling is similarly concerned with the sequencing of permissible combinations of letters to make up words. In this respect Peters has argued that spelling should be taught through what she describes as 'letter strings' – combinations of letters which when placed together make certain sounds in the language. Various activities which encourage the development of these skills include:

- Finger tracing over letters in a word while a child simultaneously sounds it out. The importance of a multi-sensory attack is emphasised by this approach.
- Combining the teaching of spelling with the development of handwriting, which can also be taught in letter strings. Peters (1985) has argued there is a strong connection between good handwriting and good spelling.
- The use of 'letter string pockets' by pupils, where the word which they had asked to be spelt was placed in the correct pocket for future use. This not only provided them with an aide memoir but also gave them a multi-sensory, physical activity in an attempt to help them remember the position the string had been placed in.
- The use of the look–cover–write–check technique was proposed by Peters and Cripps (1983) and Cripps (1983). This approach involves the child in looking at the word in question, covering it up, writing it from memory and checking it for accuracy. There are various forms in which this can be undertaken including vocabulary books with folded pages or a procedure where the teacher writes the word on a piece of paper and the child has to carry it in their memory back to their place to write it down.

Reason and Boote argue that learning to spell is complex. They emphasise the need for encouragement, enjoyment and understanding in order for children to gain success. Further, they point out the need for children to have a feeling of being a partner in control of their development in this area.

Initial strategies which are suggested by Cripps (1983), Peters (1985), and Reason and Boote (1994), indicate the importance of analysing the current work of children who appear to have difficulties. This can be done initially as a comparison between the level of ability of others in the class and in the light of the experience of the teacher with children of a similar age. This can be done also as a needs analysis relating particularly to the children's strengths, what do they know and at what stage are they in their personal development.

Reason and Boote (1994) detailed four stages in learning to spell. These equate roughly but not identically with the first three levels outlined in the National Curriculum for English.

- Stage One relates to children who have the ability to recognise rhymes and rhyming words, have some ability to blend spoken sounds into words and who have some knowledge of the initial phonic structures in the writing of words.
- Stage Two is reached when children can write single letter sounds, some commonly used words of up to four letters and they can analyse words into their constituent parts.
- Stage Three is reached when children can write words with consonant digraphs, consonant blends and vowel digraphs. At this stage they should also understand the use of the 'magic e' sound at the end of words and be able to spell most common words.
- At Stage Four children will be able to spell most words accurately and have developed skills in dictionary usage.

Children with weaknesses in spelling do not acquire skills incidentally. These need to be taught, and in many cases over taught, rigorously. Teachers will need to decide their priorities and work out their strategies to develop a systematic approach. A number of points need to be considered here.

- What needs to be done with individuals and what with the whole class? Sometimes certain general difficulties with a particular word or sound will emerge in a class. These can be dealt with collectively. When this occurs the use of a funny or odd explanation to underline the point can be very effective, as can the use of pictures. On other occasions the needs of children will be individual and will need to be tackled as such. Here again humour or some memorable approach may be useful to underline the points being made.
- A multi-sensory approach using a variety of faculties may be appropriate for some children. This can be a very lengthy routine, but short cuts will not bring satisfactory results. The more obvious of these include listening properly to the word and its component parts, following the letters as each is said, writing or copying it down, memorising it and looking carefully at its difficult parts.
- The selection of words should be practical and useful to the child. The key words to be taught should give plenty of opportunity for use in their writing.
- The correction of spelling should be undertaken carefully so that the child is not faced with a myriad of errors and teacher correction all over the page. One idea here is to focus on certain words. These could be those they are learning currently, those vital in the topic or subject area or those considered to be key common words the child should be able to spell.

THE DO's AND DON'T's OF SPELLING

Peters and Cripps (1983) produced some simple instructions for the classroom teacher. They are reproduced here in simple form.

Do's

1. Talk with pupils about how words are constructed.
2. Tell them to look carefully at words and to think about the letter pattern which is similar to those in words they know already.
3. Train them to visualise words with their eyes shut.
4. Teach them when learning a word to:
   Look at it carefully
   Cover it
   Say it
   Write it
   Check it.
5. Make sure children always write from memory.
6. Write down words they have asked for and remove them before attempting to write.
7. Help them with their handwriting.
8. Watch to see they are forming their letters properly.
9. Encourage them to be careful with their written work and to take a pride in it.

Don't's

1. Allow learning to spell to become rote learning or an unpleasant chore.
2. Think that seeing a word is the same as looking carefully at it.
3. Let them copy from a sheet of spellings without going through the look–cover–write–say–check sequence.
4. Spell out letter-by-letter words that have been asked for.
5. Let poor writers write too much on their own as free writing.
6. Allow them to form their letters incorrectly.
7. Get worried about 'slip of the pen' mistakes.
8. Let them think they are poor at spelling.

OTHER STRATEGIES TO ENCOURAGE GOOD SPELLING

There are a number of activities and strategies which have been identified to aid teachers in developing spelling skills. Some of these can often be done very effectively in small segments of a long lesson.

- The use of reduced word lists to manageable proportions for those with spelling difficulties. Bryant, Drabin and Gettinger (1981) argued that if a spelling list of twenty words is reduced to only four or five for some children this is much more manageable. A review of words learned in earlier lessons during the week helps to reinforce these also.
- An approach called 'imitation plus modelling' is recommended by Mushinski-

Fulk and Stormont-Spurgin (1995b). This approach involves the teacher spelling the word orally and children writing it. The word can then be checked. This is also done orally, with the teacher sounding out the individual letters of the word and either giving praise for a correct answer or writing the correct word.

- Mushinski-Fulk and Stormont-Spurgin also detail the 'constant time delay strategy'. This involves children spelling an appropriate word and then being shown the correct spelling. This is done a few times with what is described as a 'zero time delay'. The children observe the word during this process and are then asked to spell it again in a period of five seconds before it is shown to them again. Pupils then compare their spelling with the correct one. This is an activity which can be undertaken by pupils in pairs as well as being teacher led.

- Use approaches which children can work with on their own or in small groups. Some approaches detailed here lend themselves to this, as do computer focused activities. There are an increasing number of computer based games and approaches to help here. Check with other staff in the school or a publisher's catalogue to see what is available.

- Check they understand what rhyming words are and that they can use them.

- The use of games. These include finding words within words (particularly useful here are children's names or place names, e.g. Richard – rich and hard, or Manchester – man, chest, nest etc.), or the use of letter strings to make words. These can be taken from other words or from other sources such as suitable car registration plates. Communal hangman played on the board can also be a useful aid in spelling. Further ideas can be found in Reason and Boote (1994) and Westwood (1993).

- Be positive about corrections. With poor spellers look for the words that are spelt correctly.

- If a thematic approach is appropriate to the subject ensure there is an essential word list for the topic and that it is readily available for the class to use.

- Use what Peters (1985) described as 'rational correction techniques'. Get the pupils to look through their work and underline words they think they have spelled incorrectly. Look through the ones they have missed and concentrate on those. It is with this group of words that the children have a problem.

- Ask what the school or department policy on spelling is and follow that. Cripps (1983) argued that at secondary level that without a school policy, and it being given priority, then pupil progress is unlikely. Further, he contends that even with such a policy in place it will still be difficult and may be very time-consuming.

- Point out difficult words in your own subject area.

- For younger children the use of 'magic lines' as described by Reason and Boote (1994) can be useful. This is useful when children cannot spell all of a word they wish to use and they make a line to indicate the parts which are missing or incomplete. Care is needed here however to ensure that the number of incomplete words is not so large as to make the final piece too difficult to understand.

- Allow children to participate in the selection of the list of words to be learned. This can increase motivation and allow them to feel they are part of the decision-making process.
- Provide them with a word book or personal dictionary where they can write down key words. Use the look–cover–write–check approach to this. This book can be used to construct tests for them.

There are a number of publishers' packages available to develop spelling skills. When choosing these it is important to relate them to the age of the children and to make them age and task appropriate. You should also feel comfortable as the teacher using the material. Publishers' catalogues are a useful starting point here but much of this material, as with the equivalents in maths and reading development, is expensive.

Mushinski-Fulk and Stormont-Spurgin (1995b) argued that whatever approach is used it is important that its purpose is explained to the children using it. The importance of personal effort to aid development should also be stressed, as should the tactic of the children practising the naming of the strategical steps of any approach they are using and monitoring it carefully. Most importantly they stress that whatever approach is adopted it will need a strong element of reinforcement for the pupils. Tangible reinforcements (such as stickers, merit cards or bar charts of progress) are strongly recommended whatever the approach used, as this can only help to motivate children.

ASSESSMENT

Assessment, if used properly, can be a valuable tool to provide a sense of achievement for pupils as they develop their spelling skills. Informal assessments need to be targeted properly and clearly differentiated. This can be done in a number of ways:

- the number of words given;
- grouping children with appropriate words for each, include not only recently known words but known words;
- allowing the children to test each other on occasions;
- the use of individual progress charts to show personal development.

For some children appropriately differentiated short sentences may be dictated. This, as pointed out earlier, has major difficulties if not undertaken carefully. The Alpha to Omega series of exercise (Hornsby and Shear, 1990) is a useful source here.

On the more formal level of assessment there are a number of published tests available. These include the Diagnostic Spelling Test (Vincent and Claydon, 1981). This is a group test, basically for junior age children, which provides useful diagnostic information. Strategies for Teachers and Learners (Peters and Smith, undated, NFER Nelson) is similarly a diagnostic group spelling test. This is suitable for pupils in both primary and secondary school. There is a very useful accompanying handbook which details strategies and techniques for teaching.

DICTIONARY WORK

For those children who are reaching Stage Four detailed by Reason and Boote (1994) there is value in dictionary work. The use of a dictionary is an aid to independence. However, to use a dictionary successfully children need certain skills. These skills can be long-term developments for children and for those at the early stages of this there is need of considerable reinforcement as well as practise of new skills. The basic knowledge required to undertake this work includes knowledge of the alphabet both in terms of letter order and individual location. For older children a phonic dictionary which lists words according to their initial sound and syllable length might be appropriate. An example of this is the ACE dictionary produced by the LDA in Wisbech.

HANDWRITING

Handwriting is often a problem for children with SEN. Those with poor motor control often have untidy presentation, which is unattractive to the reader and personally unsatisfactory to the children also.

There are a number of overall difficulties. Children often mis-form letters, starting at the wrong point, and going the wrong way round to shape them. Some have little skill in joining their letters together. As with spelling, learning handwriting is not incidental – it has to be taught with care and precision.

Handwriting changes with maturation and these changes can be noted particularly around adolescence. Here, considerable changes in size of letters and the way they are formed can occur. There can also be changes which can be accounted for in differences in the mood of children or the time of day. Tired children have a tendency to write less neatly.

STRATEGIES AND APPROACHES

A number of factors need to be taken into consideration in teaching children to write and in observing their work in this area. Alston and Taylor (1987) and Reason and Boote (1994) relate good handwriting to three key factors: legibility, fluency and speed.

Legibility

These include the physical conditions: the posture of the child, the positioning of the paper and the grip on the pen or pencil. The materials they are using are also a crucial factor. This includes the implement they are using. Here, the level of skill of the children should be the key factor rather than their age. The size and style of the paper also needs to be taken into account. Ruled paper is often very difficult for infants to work with. However, Reason and Boote (1994) suggest that for formal handwriting sessions even at that age ruled paper should be used.

The size of a child's handwriting should also determine the width of the lines they are writing on. For some children with difficulties in keeping their writing on a straight line the use of guidelines under their page is encouraged.

Children should be encouraged to use tools which give the best results. The model of handwriting taught is also important. Alston and Taylor (1987) argued that those with poorer control should be taught cursive style as it is less demanding on them. There are indications that for many younger children with SEN this is a problem, and that printing continues to persist as a common approach. With older children though the cursive approach has advantages. It helps them to see words as a unit and can help in the development of both fluency and speed as well as providing them with a more adult style. This is an issue which needs careful monitoring.

Good practice in this area needs careful planning. Short exercises in small groups are preferable, with close supervision by the teacher. The training and use of classroom ancillaries might be a possibility.

To develop good skills the children need to be carefully observed as they form their letters. Practice and praise are essential. Children should practise their letter formation by repeating the same letter along a line. Developments can best be undertaken by developing skills with letters of similar shapes, rather than in straight alphabetical order.

As with spelling, a multi-sensory approach can be useful in developing handwriting skills. Reason and Boote (1994) indicate that appropriate strategies include reading the letter, watching how it is formed, tracing with the finger round it and writing it out. They indicate that neither tracing nor simply copying letters is a sound tactic.

Fluency

Exercises to aid fluency include the practice of large rhythmic patterns on paper. The size of the paper needs to be commensurate with the needs of the children, moving from large to small paper with practice. Similarly finger tracing can be a useful exercise. For those with poor muscular control fluency can be improved by the teacher discussing where children might place natural breaks in words they have written.

Speed

Speed improves with practice and in normal circumstances this should be enough. For some slower children practising letter strings may help here. Sometimes legibility and neatness may suffer as speed increases.

Both spelling and handwriting are skills which for pupils with a wide range of SEN need to be taught. This often needs to be done sequentially and with precision. They are both areas of considerable difficulty for them. It is important that they are given both time and encouragement to develop their skills.

CHAPTER 11

Developing mathematics skills

INTRODUCTION

This chapter will focus on issues relevant to the teaching of maths, particularly basic arithmetic skills, to pupils who have considerable difficulties in this area of work. These for many pupils, especially those with learning difficulties, can be related to the essentially conceptual nature of the subject. Children with SEN are easily confused by what is required by the processes of maths and may have little sense of what is expected to answer questions which have been posed. For these pupils even the apparently simplest of arithmetic tasks, such as subtraction or division, can be at a level which they find difficult without any form of tactile aids.

Issues which will be raised include the main problems pupils with SEN face, suitable approaches which will help, and an outline of an appropriate model of practice for the teacher.

DIFFICULTIES

Mathematics often appears as an abstract symbolic subject and teaching it to weaker pupils has been described by Haylock (1991) as 'one of the most difficult jobs in the world'. Nevertheless, as he also points out, it is a subject where this group of pupils can gain success and confidence. However, this may take place only slowly, over a long and sometimes frustrating period of time.

The Cockcroft Report (Cockcroft, 1982) supported the views of Piaget and others with regard to the different rates of development of pupils in attaining skills in maths. This suggests that there is a wide variation of skill, with some eleven-year-old pupils able to perform tasks expected of the average fourteen-year-old. However, others of that age are unable to perform the tasks expected of seven-year-olds.

The reasons for this disparity are based on a wide range of factors, and are dependent on the circumstances of the individual child. These can be related to cognitive or perceptual difficulties (where the concepts are too difficult for children to fully understand), poor manipulative skills, restricted concrete experiences in the concepts and ideas being taught, and breaks in the continuity of their learning (in what is essentially a sequential process).

It is bearing this in mind which makes it so important that the subject content for those pupils with difficulties should be clearly differentiated from that expected of their counterparts. This must take into account both the difference in the pace at which pupils with SEN can learn and also their lack of ability to conceptualise or to work in abstract terms. Mathematics demands this and for some pupils their lessons, if the teacher is not careful, may bout e composed of a diet of the development of arithmetical skills only. This is a prospect which would not be helpful to either party.

THE MAIN PROBLEMS

There are a number of ways in which pupils with difficulties with maths can be identified.

- Confusion in the meaning of the arithmetical signs. It is common among children who are weak mathematically at the age of eleven not to be able to recognise the division sign let alone to be able to deal with the concepts involved.
- Visual sequencing problems of the numbers in the operation. Again it is common among this group of pupils in secondary school to be unable always to copy out a sum correctly.
- Inability to transfer from the horizontal presentation of work to be done to the vertical, or visa versa.
- Difficulties with place values, not understanding the difference between hundreds and thousands or even tens and hundreds.
- Conceptual weaknesses, not being able to give a rough estimate of an answer. This shows up particularly in calculator work when the answer is wrong and the child is unable to understand why.
- The inability to be able to transfer computational skills to real life situations. The reverse of this can also be the case when some practical situation demands arithmetic skills and the child is unable to understand which skill to use to find the right answer.
- Inaccuracies in working out answers. This can be a consistent problem or one which occurs occasionally. In the first situation this may be through a lack of understanding of the skill needed. In the second this can often be through a lack of concentration by the child or forgetting the skill required through a lack of internalisation on their part.
- Inaccuracies in presentation. A number of problems occur in this respect. These include poor handwriting and figure formation which the child cannot follow and the inability to set the numbers in the question out in the correct columns. A number of children want to set out their work in the horizontal style and then find that they cannot work successfully in this mode. Often pupils who are weak at arithmetic need to write the questions out in vertical columns for greater accuracy.
- Poor vocabulary which will not allow the pupil to understand the question which has been asked.
- The readability level of the problem is too great and the child is unable to understand the language of the questions being asked. It is the case that the maths skills of those pupils with considerable reading difficulties may not be extended if they are constantly put in situations where their reading demands are too great for them.

- A poor attention span from pupils. Maths is a difficult area for concentrated effort for some pupils and for those who find the subject difficult this is an additional problem.

It is important to encourage good work habits in children and to develop their interest and competence in the subject through developing their confidence. It is vitally important that negative attitudes are not allowed to develop and thus not only hinder development but cause further behavioural difficulties.

ASSESSMENT

As with the assessment of reading skills described in Chapter 9, the assessment of mathematical skills can take two forms: formative and summative. As in Chapter 9, this section will concentrate on the diagnostic and formative assessments.

Sellinger (1994) argued that the effective testing of mathematical skills must reflect, encourage and support pupil learning. Essentially diagnostic testing must elicit from pupils:

- their level of understanding of work which has been completed;
- problems they have encountered;
- information to help in the planning of future work.

Assessing the level of mathematical skills of children with SEN is often circumspect, taking into account only the first three levels of the six stage process described by Mason (1994). It is usual that this takes the form of undertaking particular tasks in a specific context and relating this to what they have already learned.

Sellinger argued that to assess the skills of children in this subject a wide range of approaches is valuable. She indicated these should include listening, observing, questioning, discussing and interpreting the activities of pupils. This can be done either informally or formally.

INFORMAL ASSESSMENTS

Informal assessments can be very useful to maths teachers. They can show the current knowledge of children (in terms of both their strengths and weaknesses) and help to find the correct starting point for them in a topic. Further, they can be conducted in an unthreatening way which will not only prove to be more accurate but also help to boost confidence.

Such assessments can take a variety of forms. However, it is important that they are set around appropriate tasks based on what the children have been taught. They can be knowledge based, practical (such as survey work or working with shape or area), problem solving or a combination of all of these. The answers can be written, oral or aural, or a combination of these approaches. They can be directed by the teacher or undertaken as an essentially pupil-centred activity.

In respect of the work of Piaget discussed in Chapter 7, it is important to be able to ascertain at what level of mathematical thinking the children are working. In many cases, for those children with learning difficulties this will be at the initial concrete operations level of thinking, where they will be needing to deal in real terms with arithmetic issues. This may include the use of Cuisenaire Rods, fingers or a number line to find the answers to questions.

The key points in any assessment of difficulties relate to:

- What did the child get wrong?
- Why did they get it wrong?
- Is it a problem of the perception of how to address the task?
- Can children complete the task with the use of concrete examples?
- Can children explain the process which they are required to do? At which point are they not able to do this?

KEY LEVELS OF ASSESSMENT

Westwood (1993) provided a series of key steps for assessing children's mathematical skills. These, if undertaken by the teacher, will indicate the level of attainment of pupils and provide a starting point for teaching. These are arranged in three levels of ability.

The first concentrates on pre-number, vocabulary and number recognition work, as well as the elementary aspects of arithmetic skills such as working with addition and subtraction skills with numbers of less than ten.

The second level deals with issues such as addition, simple mental arithmetic tasks with numbers under twenty, and the use of both the vertical and horizontal setting out process for calculation as well as issues of telling the time and knowledge of the days in the week and months in the year.

The third level of assessment deals with pupils who have somewhat higher order skills. These include competences in the use of numbers beyond a hundred, knowledge of multiplication tables, understanding of place value, fraction recognition (in both the vulgar and decimal form) and satisfactory knowledge of working with both money and simple written problems.

FORMAL ASSESSMENTS

Formal diagnostic assessments in maths for pupils with SEN will provide either an overall quotient of ability or a profile of skill attainment. For those pupils with SEN it is often the latter of these which is the most useful and revealing.

The former type, such as the Maths 7–11 series (NFER, 1996), may be useful to provide some indication of performance when compared with national standards or as part of the setting process for the maths department in a secondary school. However, this type of assessment will not always indicate the level of skill shown by the child and as such will not provide the starting point at which teaching should begin. Tests which will do this include Yardsticks, Criterion Referenced Tests in Mathematics (Yardsticks, 1975) and the Profile of

Mathematical Skills (France, 1979). As with reading tests, mathematics tests need to take into account the actual age of the children completing them. Publishers' catalogues will provide the correct information for this.

WORKING WITH THE NATIONAL CURRICULUM

The National Curriculum specifies very clearly what children, unless they have been disapplied, are expected to work on. The list is wide ranging and includes measuring, weight, capacity, shape and area and fractions. More detail can be gained from looking at the relevant sections of the National Curriculum documentation.

The Non Statutory Guidance from the National Curriculum Council (1989b) provided some guidelines on the approaches which may be appropriate.

- Balancing activities between those of a short-term duration and others where there is scope for longer term work.
- Ensuring that the activities are balanced between independent and cooperative work.
- Setting tasks where there is a balance between exact results and many possible outcomes.
- Employing different approaches to learning. These include observations, talking and listening, discussion with other pupils, reflecting on activities completed, drafting and reading and writing.
- Ensuring that pupils are able to develop their personal qualities.
- Activities which enable the pupils to develop a positive attitude to maths.

CLASSROOM MANAGEMENT STRATEGIES

There are a number of models (e.g. Bailey, 1982; Haylock, 1991; Aherne, 1993) which indicate appropriate approaches for pupils with SEN, particularly those with learning difficulties. That provided by Bailey is a particularly useful overall approach. He argued that any approach must take into account the following issues:

- *Defining* the aims and objectives for the pupils in the lessons.
- *Assessing* the pupils, using a variety of different approaches including normative and criterion referenced material, informal observations and error analysis.
- *Planning* the teaching programme and present learning experiences through a range of materials, strategies and organisational features.
- *Evaluating* the teaching programme through ongoing assessment of pupils' progress.

PROVIDING HELP

For pupils with difficulties in maths Westwood (1993) argues for a balanced approach to teaching, where there is a considerable focus on explicit teaching accompanied by 'hands on' experience. He further argued that the discovery method and both group and collaborative learning approaches are less efficient for those with difficulties in this subject.

Ablewhite (1969) indicated there are key principles to be taken into consideration when teaching maths to weaker pupils. These are related to pace, awareness, vocabulary and the concept of number, motivation, presentation, and readability and vocabulary.

Pace Children learn at different speeds and in different ways. With this in mind teachers must provide useful and enjoyable tasks rather than setting pre-determined goals to be met by the end of the term. It is also important that pupils are not allowed to become bored. With this in mind, Westwood (1993) points out the importance of teacher awareness concerning the pace with which material is presented to a child. This is vital so that the child can assimilate the skills and concepts properly before moving on to new material.

Awareness Ensure that the children are properly aware of what they have been doing. This will help them to remember more clearly the things they have learned.

Vocabulary Ensure that the child's vocabulary is developed to the point where there is a good understanding of the terms which are essential to both learning and understanding. Where there is a language deficiency work will need to be done in this area.

The concept of number For children with SEN it is important to work on their concept of number and their basic arithmetic skills for a large extent of the time. However, do not expect progress to be quick. For many pupils with SEN the concepts of arithmetic, let alone mathematics, are a mystery and it may take a long and painstaking effort from both them and you before the 'fog' begins to lift. The use of a revisiting approach with key teaching points being revisited and revised regularly is recommended by Dempster (1991) and Westwood (1993).

Motivation It is important in maths, as in other areas of the curriculum, that the content of lessons helps to motivate the children. This can operate in two clearly defined ways. Firstly, the content of lessons can be seen by the pupils as directly relevant to their future needs on either a personal or social level. Since aspects of the maths curriculum clearly lend themselves very easily to this, it is important that this is used by the teacher whenever possible. Secondly, there are aspects of the maths curriculum that pupils find intrinsically interesting and will work at with considerable motivation. These aspects of course vary from child to child and it is an important part of the teacher's management skills to find out about their interests and to concentrate for a considerable proportion of their teaching time on these.

Presentation When presenting work to pupils with learning difficulties in maths the layout of the material can be crucially important. An attractive page of work will act to motivate children. Bearing this in mind it is important that the material should be presented attractively with illustrations and diagrams. It is important to avoid small print. This is not helpful to those with reading difficulties and can cause particular difficulties for pupils with sight problems. It is also important to avoid close spacing of lines and heavy blocks of written text as they are particularly off-putting to pupils with SEN.

Readability and vocabulary Similarly the question of the readability of the material is important. Pupils with difficulties in maths often have difficulties with reading and writing. It is important to avoid long complicated sentences, uncommon words and multi-syllabic and irregular words. Time can be fruitfully spent on talking over both the vocabulary of the text that is presented and the instructions for completing the work and to check on any ambiguities which may arise.

Experience helps to indicate which mathematical terms will cause the most difficulties but a good rule of thumb is to explain and discuss fully any new terms which may crop up. In this respect it is also a valuable exercise to look at the vocabulary which has been used and to see which, if any, could be simplified or omitted altogether.

The content of maths lessons needs to be kept simple. Bearing in mind all the points made above, children will easily be confused if there are complicated instructions or concepts to be handled and learned. It is important to remember that the number of variables that a child can handle is determined by their intellectual ability. Haylock (1991) suggested that for those pupils with SEN, maths should be taught in carefully sequenced stages.

CHAPTER 12

Working with parents

INTRODUCTION

Establishing constructive working relationships with parents is a key element of meeting the educational needs of all children but it is particularly important for those children with SEN. This is because parents of children with SEN are likely to require greater support and guidance than many other parents and also because there are many ways in which such parents can help teachers to provide the most effective education for their children. This chapter will consider what teachers need to know and do in order to work in partnership with parents. First, a model for understanding different aspects of parental involvement will be presented. Then, various strategies which teachers can use to establish and maintain effective communication with parents will be described.

A MODEL FOR WORKING WITH PARENTS

A model which illustrates the various aspects which teachers need to address when working with parents is presented in Figure 9. The model consists of two pyramids, one representing a hierarchy of parents' needs, the other a hierarchy of parents' strengths or possible contributions. Both pyramids demonstrate visually the different levels of needs and contributions of parents. Thus, while all parents have some needs and some potential contributions which can be utilised, a smaller number have intense need for guidance, or the capability of making an extensive contribution. The model also shows that, for parents' needs at a higher level, more time and expertise is required by teachers in order to meet these needs.

Each of the components of the model will now be outlined and teachers' roles in each of these discussed.

Needs of parents

Communication

All parents need to have effective channels of communication with the teachers who work directly with their children. They need information about the organisation and requirements of the school as it effects their children. They need to know how their children are progressing and about any assessments, reviews or changes of placement which are being considered. That is, all parents need to know about their rights and responsibilities. This can be provided through handbooks or regular newsletters written especially for parents.

	Parental contributions
Some	**Policy** PTA, Parent Governors
Many	**Resource** classroom aide, fund-raising
Most	**Collaboration** home–school reading programmes
All	**Information** children's strengths and weaknesses
All	**Communication** telephoning, newsletters for parents
Most	**Liaison** home–school diaries, parent–teacher meetings
Many	**Education** individual guidance, parent workshops
Some	**Support** support groups, counselling
	Parental needs

Figure 9 A model for working with parents

Parents need to feel that they can contact the school at any time when they have a concern about their child. Some parents prefer to communicate by telephone, others would rather call in to see the teacher face to face, while others find that contact through written notes or home–school diaries suits them best. Therefore, teachers need to ensure that a wide range of communication options are open to parents. However, the most important factor in maintaining good communication is the openness to parents which schools demonstrate through their contacts with parents. The attitude of choice has often been referred to as an 'open door policy' in which parents feel comfortable about contacting or going into the school when they have a concern. The key element of this policy is the teacher's willingness to establish and maintain open communication with parents.

Liaison

Most parents want to know how their children are getting on at school. They want to find out what their children have achieved and whether they are having any difficulties. They regard teachers as the main source of information on their children's performance at school and therefore need to have a working partnership with them. Teachers can facilitate this by keeping in regular contact with parents through such means as telephone calls, home visits, home–school notebooks, weekly report forms and by meeting with parents at school (for a detailed discussion of these forms of liaison see Hornby, 1995).

Teachers are often disappointed that some parents do not come to parent–teacher meetings at school, thereby giving the impression that they are not interested in how their children are getting on. However, there are usually other reasons for them not turning up, such as the difficulties involved in getting a babysitter, the overwhelming demands of looking after their family, or anxieties about coming to the school which are related to their own negative school experiences. It is important then, for teachers to find other ways of liaising with these parents, perhaps by having regular telephone contacts or home visits.

Education

Many parents appreciate receiving guidance from teachers on promoting their children's progress or dealing with specific difficulties. In fact, they are much more likely to approach teachers, who are in daily contact with their children, than headteachers or educational psychologists who they may see as more threatening. Class teachers are in an excellent position to provide parents with such guidance. They are knowledgeable about child development and learning and see children on a daily basis, so have the chance to get to know them well and identify any changes in behaviour or difficulties in learning which they may experience. Therefore, opportunities for receiving such guidance, or what is in effect parent education, should be freely available to all parents.

A particularly effective format for parent education is one which combines guidance about promoting children's development with opportunities for parents to discuss their concerns. Parent education programmes which involve a group of parents, and employ a workshop format, easily lend themselves to providing a combination of educational input and sharing of concerns. This type of format enables parents to learn new skills and gain confidence through talking to other parents and teachers.

Support

Some parents of children with SEN, at some times, are in need of supportive counselling, even though they may not actually request it. This support can be provided either individually by teachers, educational psychologists or social workers, or in groups such as self-help groups or support groups. Although such support should be available to all parents, the majority of parents seldom need extensive counselling. In the past it has often been assumed that the greatest need of parents of children with SEN is counselling in order to help them come to terms with their child's disability. This has led to an overemphasis on this aspect of parent involvement to the detriment of the other aspects, such as communication and liaison, which have been discussed above. The fact is that if parents have good channels of communication and regular liaison with teachers, coupled with the opportunity to receive guidance about their children whenever they need it, then only a very few of them will need extensive counselling at any particular time.

Whereas most British parents are reluctant to seek the help of professional counsellors, they will approach their children's teachers in search of guidance or counselling for the problems which concern them. Teachers should therefore have a level of basic counselling skills sufficient to be good listeners and to help parents solve everyday problems (see Hornby, 1994). They should also be able to refer parents on to professional counsellors or support groups when problems raised are beyond their level of competence.

Parents' contributions

Information

All parents can contribute valuable information about their children because they have known them throughout their lives and have been the ones who have participated in all previous contacts with professionals in order to assess and plan for meeting their children's needs. Information concerning children's likes and dislikes, strengths and weaknesses, along with any relevant medical details can be gathered by teachers at parent–teacher meetings. Many parents feel more comfortable on their own territory and generally appreciate it when teachers offer to visit them. This also provides an opportunity to observe how parents cope with their children at home and to learn about any relevant family circumstances. Making full use of parents' knowledge of their children not only leads to more effective teaching, it also makes parents feel that they have been listened to and that an active interest has been taken in their children.

Collaboration

Most parents are willing and able to contribute more than just information. Most parents are able to collaborate with teachers by reinforcing classroom programmes at home in activities ranging from checking homework diaries to conducting home–school reading or behavioural programmes. However, while involvement in such schemes should always be offered to all parents, including those who have not collaborated in the past, it should be accepted that a small proportion of parents will not be able participate for a variety of justifiable reasons. The class teacher's role is to optimise levels of collaboration for the maximum number of parents.

Resource

Many parents have the time and ability to act as voluntary teacher aides, either assisting in the classroom or in the preparation of materials, or in fund-raising.

Others may have special skills which they can contribute such as helping prepare newsletters, in craft activities, or in curriculum areas in which they have a special talent. In these times of contracting professional resources teachers should make sure that they make optimum use of this valuable voluntary resource. Therefore invitations for parents to help at the school need to be sent out at least annually by such means as newsletters.

Policy

Some parents are able to contribute their expertise through membership of parent or professional organisations. This includes being a school governor, a lay inspector, a member of the PTA, or being involved in a parent support or advocacy group. Others have the time and ability to provide in-service training for teachers. Parents can influence school policy on children with special needs through their involvement as a governor or PTA member. They can also sometimes influence government policy on children with special educational needs through their involvement in groups such as MENCAP and SCOPE (formerly The Spastics Society). Therefore teachers should continually be on the look out for parents who can contribute in these ways so that their abilities can be used to the full.

COMMUNICATING WITH PARENTS

There are five main methods for developing and maintaining two-way communication between parents and teachers. These are informal contacts, various forms of written communication, telephone contacts, parent–teacher meetings, and home visits. These are now discussed in turn, starting with informal contacts. Detailed guidelines for each of the five methods of communication with parents are described elsewhere (Hornby, 1995).

Informal contacts

Typical forms of informal contacts are school productions which involve the child with SEN, open days, gala days, and educational visits in the community. Such informal contacts are a useful way of 'breaking the ice' in most forms of human relationships and this is also the case in relationships with parents. Such contacts provide a means whereby parents and teachers can meet each other as people with a mutual interest in building relationships on behalf of children, thereby helping to break down the barriers that often exist between school and home. Informal contacts are particularly important for parents of children newly enrolled at the school or when there has not been a high level of parent involvement at the school in the past. In the latter situation teachers understandably become despondent when the attendance at more formal events, such as parents' evenings, is so poor. When this is the case it is often best to organise informal events in order to increase the numbers of parents having contact with the school and thereby establish the context necessary for the development of other forms of contact.

Written communication

Many parents prefer to communicate with teachers by means of letters. Other parents find that home–school diaries are the best means of keeping them in contact with the school. In addition, newsletters and handbooks written especially for parents of children with SEN can keep parents in touch with what is happening at school. Progress reports are also used to maintain communication with parents. It is therefore clear that the written word provides an important means of communication between teachers and parents.

However, there are two major difficulties with this form of communication. First, if some of the pupils' parents do not have English as their first language then ideally every written communication to parents needs to be translated into their own languages. Second, it is important to remember that some parents have reading difficulties themselves. Therefore, written materials cannot be relied upon to communicate effectively with all parents. This also suggests that all written materials should use language which is simple and able to be understood by the majority of parents.

Telephone contacts

Some parents prefer to communicate with teachers by means of the telephone. Many parents appreciate the opportunity of being able to phone teachers directly either at school or at home. However, there are difficulties associated with both of these options. The main problem with parents phoning teachers at school is that teachers should only have to leave their class to answer the telephone in absolute emergencies. So it is best to get the school secretary take messages and tell parents that the teacher will phone back as soon a possible. Also, many teachers may not be prepared to allow parents to phone them at home. This is perfectly understandable since they may feel the need to have some time to themselves, or with their own families, which work pressures do not impinge on. An alternative solution is to set a specified time during the week when parents know the teacher will be available to answer the phone.

Alternatively, teachers may prefer to contact parents by telephone rather than by sending a letter. It is useful to check whether some parents are at home during the day and whether others are happy to be phoned at work, in which case such calls can be made from school during the day.

Parent–teacher meetings

The form of contact with parents with which all teachers are familiar is that of parents' evenings or parent–teacher meetings. These meetings are a well established method of involving parents and not without reason, as research has shown that they have an impact on both parent–teacher relationships and pupil progress. It has been found that children whose parents attend such meetings have higher attendance rates, fewer behaviour problems and improved academic achievement. Of course experienced teachers would immediately suggest that this is because the parents of 'good kids' usually attend parents' evenings whereas parents of pupils with behavioural or learning difficulties tend not to turn up. However, it must not be assumed that parents who do not turn up to parents' evenings are not interested in their children's education. There are a variety of reasons why some parents do not attend such meetings, including transport and babysitting problems, as well as parents' negative feelings about their own school days. Perhaps if these problems could be overcome then these parents would come to parents' evenings and this would lead to better parent–teacher relationships and thereby an improvement in their children's progress at school. I believe that it would, but it is usually easier to use other strategies to communicate with these parents to overcome the problems. By using either home visits, telephone contacts or written communication, good parent–teacher relationships can be established which should lead to improvements in children's behaviour and academic progress.

Home visits

Many parents appreciate it when their children's teachers are prepared to come and visit them on their own territory. Such home visits can be pivotal in establishing close working relationships with parents. They enable teachers to see for themselves the circumstances in which the family are living. They also enable teachers to meet other members of the family such as siblings and fathers who they may not otherwise meet. Knowledge of these factors can help teachers understand how their pupils may be affected by the home situation.

Home visits also enable teachers to find out how their pupils spend their time at home, whether they have any hobbies, how much television they watch and what time they usually go to bed. It is also possible to find out how pupils behave at home and how their parents handle them. Finally, home visits provide an opportunity for teachers to answer parents' questions and deal with any concerns they may have.

CHAPTER 13

Whole-school issues

INTRODUCTION

There are a number of issues relating to the provision for pupils with SEN which affect the whole school and the way that it operates. These are issues which will need to be addressed through the development of a whole-school SEN policy. The Code of Practice on the Identification and Assessment of Special Educational Needs (DfE, 1994b) and Circular 6/94 (DfE, 1994a) set out the guidelines as to what this should include. This chapter will briefly detail these requirements and discuss other factors which the school should also take into account in its development of good practice for those with SEN.

THE WHOLE-SCHOOL SEN POLICY

The guidelines for the implementation of the whole-school policy on SEN must address a wide range of issues.

- The principles and objectives which determine the policy and provision.
- The name of the school coordinator responsible for its day-to-day management.
- The arrangements to ensure that the practices and responsibilities detailed are well coordinated.
- The admission arrangements for pupils with SEN.
- Details of any special facilities or expertise which can be offered in the school.
- The arrangements made to allow physical accessibility to the school.
- The principles by which the resource allocation is made.
- The organisation of provision to identify, assess, monitor and review the progress of pupils with SEN.
- Arrangements made to allow access to a broad, balanced and relevant curricular programme.
- The approaches used to allow for the integration of pupils to participate as fully as possible in all school activities.
- The processes used for the evaluation of the school practices and procedures.
- The arrangements in place for dealing with complaints.
- The plans for staff development and in-service training.
- The arrangements for asking for professional support from outside the school.
- A description of the arrangements made for developing partnerships with parents.
- Details of links, either through staff or pupil participation, with other schools.
- Details of links with outside agencies.

It is not the purpose of this book to deal with these features in detail and they have been summarised only. The Code of Practice and Circular 6/94 provide further details of the content for such a policy. Hornby, Davis and Taylor (1995) discussed the strategies for its development, and also provided examples of appropriate approaches to its implementation.

The school is required to have a policy document on SEN and this should be available in schools for parents and other interested parties. It is advisable to acquaint yourself with it. The school coordinator should be able to provide you with a copy.

RESPONSIBILITIES OF THE CLASSROOM TEACHER

The Code of Practice also detailed guidelines for the roles of the major partners in schools – the governors, the headteacher and the staff – in discharging their responsibilities to those children with SEN. The governors, along with the headteacher, retain overall control of the policy which is adopted in the school. The headteacher may, in some schools, delegate the day-to-day responsibilities to the SENCO. The Code of Practice is not prescriptive and each school will determine its policy for SEN. Although many of them will be similar across the country, each school can have its individual approaches to meet its own particular needs at each stage of the process. It is important therefore that teachers are aware of the mechanisms which have been put in place. However, it may be useful at this point to indicate the main responsibilities of the class or subject teacher at each of the five stages.

Stage 1
As detailed in Chapter 1, the teacher has a key responsibility at Stage 1 of the process in identifying children with special educational needs and informing the coordinator of their concerns. Their responsibilities however do no stop there. Beyond Stage 1 these are shared with others in the school. However, class teachers continue to play a vital role in the process.

Stage 2
At Stage 2 the teacher has some responsibility, along with the SENCO, for drawing up the Individual Education Plans (IEPs) for those children who have reached this stage. They also have a responsibility to implement and monitor these for the children in their class. Some schools have a prepared format for IEPs, which often need, in part at least, to be completed by the class teacher.

It is also important that the SENCO is kept informed of the progress of children. This is particularly important at the time of review meetings so that decisions can be made on the most up to date information.

Stage 3
At Stage 3 the class teacher will be working with the IEP which has been drawn up for those children at this stage. The processes involved are similar to those described for Stage 2 above.

Stage 4
At this point the LEA will consider the need for a statutory assessment of children. As part of this process schools will be asked to submit advice. Teachers should be asked for their views on the progress of children who are being considered for a formal assessment and be kept informed of any progress which has been made.

Stage 5
Those children who have reached this stage have received a Statement of Special Educational Need. This is a legal document and schools (usually through the SENCO) have the responsibility to ensure that the provision detailed on it is arranged and monitored. As part of this process the SENCO must ensure that class teachers are aware of the provisions of the Statement and are familiar with the appropriate teaching strategies and resources to meet them.

INDIVIDUAL EDUCATION PLANS

Part of the processes identified in the Code of Practice relate to the use of Individual Education Plans with pupils who are at Stage 2 or beyond of the process. The Code of Practice (p.28) details seven areas which must be addressed. Among these the plans are used to set specific learning targets for individual children over a pre-determined period of time. For certain children there will be a whole series of targets across the curriculum areas on a rolling programme. The length of each programme is set by the SENCO, or the member of staff given responsibility for this.

Each stage of the IEP will be completed with a review of the achievements made and the strategies used. In setting new targets, the strategies to achieve these should also be discussed as should the approaches to assessing and monitoring further progress.

The overall responsibility for the coordination of these plans lies with the SENCO in the school. However, the responsibility for determining the targets and the strategies to be used to teach and monitor progress in many lessons lies with the classroom teacher. For those with little experience in this area the situation may appear daunting.

In practice the SENCO and the special needs teaching staff should provide help and guidance. They should be approached if this is needed. Help may also be available if the child has a learning support teacher who visits on a regular basis. However this will only be the case if the child has triggered concerns which have led to Stage 3 of the process.

OTHER WHOLE-SCHOOL ISSUES

It is likely that schools will also have developed 'whole-school' policies on a number of other issues. These might include bullying, discipline, assessment or curriculum planning. In such circumstances the individual teacher can expect to work in cooperation with other colleagues in designing and implementing appropriate strategies.

One example of this is the responsibility of translating the principles of entitlement indicated in the Warnock Report (DES, 1978) and other DES documents (see DES, 1984, 1988, 1989) into daily provision for all pupils. For those with SEN the key area to be addressed is the development plan for individual subject areas to take into account their learning needs.

Similarly all staff need to be informed and involved in developing a whole-school assessment procedure. This will have common features relating to the overall curriculum planning and both the formal and informal assessment procedures. Currently this will have to take into account the requirements of both the external assessment and examination agencies.

Whole-school issues are precisely that and the whole school staff, not only the teachers, might expect to be involved in the discussions which take place and the policy decisions which are made. The mechanisms for this vary greatly in individual schools, as do the topics which are considered. It is essential that you familiarise yourself with these.

BIBLIOGRAPHY

Ablewhite, R.C. (1969) *Mathematics and the Less Able.* London: Heinemann.

Aherne, P. (1993) *Mathematics for All.* London: David Fulton Publishers.

Alston, J. and Taylor, J. (1987) *Handwriting: Theory, Research and Practice.* London: Croom Helm.

Anderson, E.M. and Spain, B. (1977) *The Child with Spina Bifida.* London: Methuen.

Audit Commission/HMI (1992) *Getting in on the Act: Provision for pupils with Special Educational Needs. The National Picture.* London: DfE/HMSO.

Ayers, H., Clarke, D. and Murray, A. (1995) *Perspectives on Behaviour. A practical Guide to Effective Intervention by Teachers.* London: David Fulton Publishers.

Bailey, T. (1982) 'Mathematics in the Secondary School', in M. Hinson and M. Hughes (eds) *Planning Effective Progress.* Amersham: Hulton/NARE.

Ball, S.J. (1981) *Beachside Comprehensive.* Cambridge: Cambridge University Press.

Barthorpe, T. and Visser, J. (1991) *Differentiation, Your Responsibility – an in-service pack for staff development.* Stafford: NARE.

Bernstein, B. (1970) 'Pedagogies Visible and Invisible', in J. Karabil and A.H. Halsey (eds) *Power and Ideology in Education.* Oxford: Oxford University Press.

Best, A.B. (1992) *Teaching Children with Visual Impairments.* Milton Keynes: Open University Press.

Booth, T., Swann, W., Masterson, M. and Potts, P. (1992) *Learning for All (2) Policies for Diversity in Education.* London: Routledge.

Brennan, W.K. (1985) *Curriculum for Special Needs.* Milton Keynes: Open University Press.

British Epilepsy Association (undated) *A Guide for Teachers.* London: British Epilepsy Association.

Bryant , N.D., Drabin, I.R. and Gettinger, M. (1981) 'Effect of varying unit size on spelling achievement in learning disabled children', *Journal of Learning Disabilities,* **14**, pp.200–3.

Cameron, R.J. (1986) *Portage, pre-schools: Parents and Professionals.* Windsor: NFER Nelson.

Chapman, E.K. and Stone, J.M. (1988) *The Visually Handicapped Child in your Classroom.* London: Cassell.

Child, D. (1993) *Psychology and the Teacher.* Eastbourne: Holt Reinhardt and Winston.

Cockcroft, W.H. (1982) (Chair) *Mathematics Counts.* Report of the Committee of Enquiry into the teaching of Mathematics in schools. London: HMSO.

Cohen, L. and Manion L. (1992) *A Guide to Teaching Practice.* London Routledge.

Cooper, P. (1994) *Effective Schools for Disaffective Children.* London: Routledge.

Cripps, C.C. (1983) 'A report on an experiment to see whether young children can be taught to write from memory', *Remedial Education,* **18**, 1.

Croucher, N. (1988) *Outdoor Pursuits for Disabled People.* Cambridge: Woodhead Faulkner.

Darsborough, A. and Kinrade, J. (eds) (1981) *Directory for the Disabled,* Third edition. London: RADAR.

Davie, R., Butler, N. and Goldstein, H. (1972) *From Birth to Seven.* London: Longman.

Dearing, R. (1993) *The National Curriculum and its Assessment: Final Report.* London: National Curriculum Council and School Examination and Assessment Council.

Dempster, F.N. (1991) 'Synthesis of research on assessment and tests', *Educational Leadership,* **48**, 7, pp.71–6.

Department for Education (1994a) *Circular 6/94.* London: DfE.

Department for Education (1994b) *Code of Practice on the Identification and Assessment of Special Educational Needs*. London: Central Office of Information.

Department of Education and Science (1978) *Meeting Special Educational Needs (The Warnock Report)*. London: HMSO.

Department of Education and Science (1988) *Educational Reform Act Bulletin, Issue 4*. London: HMSO.

Department of Education and Science (1989a) *A Curriculum for All*. London: HMSO.

Department of Education and Science (1989b) *Circular 5/89*. London: HMSO.

Department of Education and Science (1994) *Parents Charter, Children with Special Needs*. London: DES.

Doch, E.W. (1954) *A Manual for Remedial Reading*. London: Garrard Press.

Galloway, D. (1995) 'Truancy, delinquency and disruption: differential school influences?', *British Psychological Society Education Section Review*, **2**, pp.49–53.

Halliday, P. (1989) *Children with Physical Difficulties*. London: Cassell.

Hargreaves, D.H. (1967) *Social Relations in the Secondary School*. London: Routledge and Kegan Paul.

Haring, N.G. and Eaton, M.D. (1978) 'Systematic instructional procedures: an instructional hierarchy', in N.G. Haring *et al*. *The Fourth R: Research in the Classroom*. Ohio: Charles E Merill.

Haskell, M. and Barrett, E. (1993) *The Education of Children with Physical and Neurological Difficulties*. London: Chapman and Hall.

Haylock, D. (1991) *Teaching Mathematics to Low Attainers 8–12*. London: Paul Chapman Publishing.

Hornby, G. (1994) *Counselling in Child Disability: Skills for Working with Parents*. London: Chapman and Hall.

Hornby, G. (1995) *Working with Parents of Children with Special Needs*. London: Cassell.

Hornby, G., Davis, G. and Taylor, G. (1995) *The Special Educational Needs Co-ordinators Handbook. A Guide for Implementing the Code of Practice*. London: Routledge.

Hornsby, B. and Shear, F. (1990) *Alpha to Omega*. London: Heinemann.

Hunt, J., McV,. Kirk, J.H. and Leiberman, C. (1975) Social Class and pre-School Language Skills (iv) Semantic Mastery of Shapes. Genetic Psychology Monographs, 91.

Hutt, E. (1986) *Teaching Language to Disordered Children: A Structured Approach*. London: Edward Arnold.

Kersner, M. and Wright, J.A. (1996) *How to Manage Communication Problems in Young Children*. London: David Fulton Publishers.

Kyriacou, C. (1991) *Essential Teaching Skills*. Oxford: Blackwell.

Lansdown, R. (1980) *More than Sympathy*. London: Tavistock.

McManus, M. (1989) *Troublesome Behaviour in the Classroom*. London: Routledge.

McNamara, S. and Moreton, G. (1995) *Changing Behaviour – Teaching Children with Emotional and Behavioural Difficulties in Primary and Secondary Classrooms*. London: David Fulton Publishers.

Macintosh, H.G. and Hale, D.E. (1976) *Assessment and the Secondary School Teacher*. London: Routledge and Kegan Paul.

Male, J. and Thomson, C. (1985) *The Educational Implications of Disability*. London: RADAR.

Martin, D. and Miller, C. (1995) *Speech and Language Difficulties in the Classroom*. London: David Fulton Publishers.

Mason, J. (1994) 'Assessing what sense pupils make of Mathematics', in M. Sellinger (ed.)

Teaching Mathematics. London: Routledge.

Miller, C. (1996) 'Sound Sense', *Special*, Spring, pp.20–24.

Mitchell, C. and Koshy, V. (1993) *Effective Teacher Assessment. Looking at children's learning in the primary classroom*. London: Hodder and Stoughton.

Moore, M. and Wade, B. (1995) *Supporting Readers – School and Classroom Strategies*. London: David Fulton Publishers.

Mortimore, P. (1980) 'The Study of Secondary Schools: A Researcher's Reply', *Perspectives*, 1 (Exeter School of Education).

Mortimore, J. and Blackstone, T. (1982) *Disadvantage and Education*. Aldershot: Gower.

Mushinski-Fulk, B. and Stormont-Spurgin, M. (1995a) 'Spelling Interventions for students with learning difficulties: review', *Journal of Special Education*, **28**, pp.488–513.

Mushinski-Fulk, B. and Stormont-Spurgin, M. (1995b) 'Fourteen spelling strategies for students with learning difficulties', *Intervention in School and Clinic*, **31**, 1, pp.16–20.

National Curriculum Council (1989a) *National Curriculum Assessment Arrangements*. York: NCC.

National Curriculum Council (1989b) *Non Statutory Guidance*. York: NCC.

Newsom, P. (1963) (CHAIR) *Half Our Future*. A Report for the Central Advisory Council for Education (England). London: HMSO.

Peters, M. (1985) *Spelling: Caught or Taught*. London: Routledge and Kegan Paul.

Peters, M. and Cripps, C.C. (1983) *Appraisal of Current Spelling Materials*. Reading: Centre for the Teaching of Reading, University of Reading.

Postlethwaite, K. and Denton, C. (1978) Streams for the Future? The Long-term Effects of Early Streaming and Non-Streaming. The Final Report of the Banbury Enquiry. Banbury: Banpubco.

Pressley, M., Burkell, J., Cariglia-Bull, T., Lysynchuk, L., McGoldrick, J.A., Schneider, B., Snyder, B.L., Symons, S. and Woloshyn, V.E. (1990) *Cognitive Strategy Instruction that Really Improves Children's Academic Performance*. Cambridge, Mass.: Brookline Books.

Pulling, D. (1977) *The Child with Cerebral Palsy*. Windsor: NFER.

Pumfrey, P.D. (1991) *Improving Children's Reading in the Junior School*. London: Cassell.

Reason, R. and Boote, R. (1994) *Helping Children with Reading and Spelling*. London: Routledge.

Reynolds, A. (1992) 'What is competent beginning teaching? A Review of the literature', *Review of Educational Research*, **62**, 1, pp.1–35.

Rosenthal, R. and Jacobson, L. (1968) *Pygmalion in the Classroom. Teacher Expectation and Pupil's Intellectual Development*. New York: Holt Rinehart and Winston.

Rutter, M., Maughan, B., Mortimore, P., Ouston, J.W. and Smith, A. (1979) *15,000 Hours, Secondary Schools and their effects on Children*. Shepton Mallet: Open Books.

Sellinger, M. (1994) Assessing in Mathematics. Teaching Mathematics in the Secondary School Mathematics Document, 7. Milton Keynes: Open University Press.

Sherliker, A. (1993) 'Integration into Mainstream Schools', *Special*, Spring, pp.38–43.

Shipman, M. (1980) 'The Limits of Positive Discrimination', M. Marland (ed.) *Education for the Inner City*. London: Heinemann.

Solity, J. and Raybould, E. (1988) *A Teacher's Guide to Special Needs*. Milton Keynes: Open University Press.

Special Educational Needs Training Consortium (1996) *Professional Development to Meet Special Educational Needs. A Report to the DfEE*. London: SENTC.

Stakes, J.R. (1987) 'The process of education and the effects on the academically less successful pupil', *School Organisation*, **8**, 1.

Stakes, J.R. (1990) The Effects of the Warnock Report and the Subsequent Legislation on the Organisation and Provision for Pupils with Special Educational Needs in the

Mainstream Secondary School. Unpublished Ph.D. Thesis. University of Hull.

Teacher Training Agency (1994) Profile of Teacher Competences – Consultations on Draft Guidance. London: Teacher Training Agency.

Thomas, G. (1985) 'Extra people in the classroom, key to integration?', *Education and Child Psychology*, **2**, iii, pp.102–7.

Tizard, J. (1981) *Involving Parents and Teachers in Nursery Schools*. London: Graw Mcintyre.

Tizard, B. and Hughes, M. (1984) *Young Children Learning*. London: Fontana.

Tomlinson, S. (1982) *A Sociology of Special Education*. London: Routledge and Kegan Paul.

Tough, J. (1977) *Development of Meaning*. London: Allen and Unwin.

Webster, A., Came, F., Webster, V. and Price, G. (1996) *Supporting Learning in the Secondary School*. Bristol: Avec Designs.

Webster, A. and Elwood, J. (1985) *The Hearing Impaired Child in the Ordinary School*. Beckenham: Croom Helm.

Webster, A. and McConnell, C. (1989) *Children with Speech and Language Difficulties*. London: Cassell.

Webster, A. and Wood, D. (1989) *Children with Hearing Difficulties*. London: Cassell.

Westwood, P. (1993) *Commonsense Methods in Special Education*. London: Routledge.

Wheldall, K. (1991) 'Managing Troublesome Classroom Behaviour in Regular Schools', *International Journal of Disability, Development and Education*, **38**, 2, pp.99–116.

Wheldall, K. and Merrett, F. (1991) *The Positive Teaching Packages*. Cheltenham Positive Products.

Willis, P. (1977) *Learning to Labour: How Working Class Boys get Working Class Jobs*. London: Saxon House.

Wolfendale, S. (1993) *Assessing Special Educational Needs*. London: Cassell.

ASSESSMENT MATERIALS

The Aston Index (1976). Windsor: National Federation for Education Research.

Brimer, M.A. and Gross. H. (1972) *The Widespan Reading Test*. London: Nelson.

Burt, C. *Rearranged Word Reading Test*. London: Hodder and Stoughton.

Dunn (undated) British Picture Vocabulary Scale.

France, N. (1979) *Profile of Mathematical Skills*. London: Nelson.

McLeod, J. and Unwin, D. (1970) *Gap Reading Comprehension Test*. London: Heinneman.

Murray McNally List (1971) (forms the basis of the Ladybird Reading Scheme, Murray, 1969).

Neale, M.D. (1958) The Neale Analysis of Reading Ability. Second edition. London: Macmillan.

National Foundation for Educational Research (1990) Maths 7-11. Windsor: NFER.

Peters, M.L. and Smith, B. (undated) *Spelling in Context: Strategies for Teachers and Learners*. Windsor: NFER Nelson.

Schonell, F.J. (1945) *Graded Reading Test*. London: Oliver and Boyd.

Vincent, D. and Claydon, J. (1981) *Diagnostic Spelling Test*. Windsor: National Foundation for Educational Research.

Yardsticks, Criterion Referenced Tests in Mathematics (1975). London: Nelson.

Young, D. (1976) *The SPAR Test*. Buckhurst Hill: Hodder and Stoughton.

Index